THE CELTIC
LUNAR ZODIAC

How to Interpret Your Moon Sign

D0572429

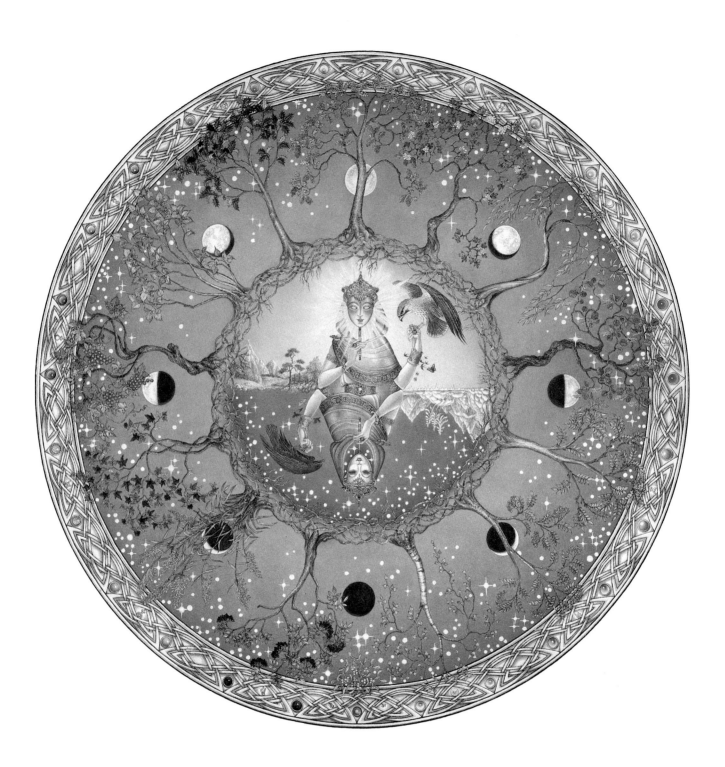

THE CELTIC LUNAR ZODIAC

How to Interpret Your Moon Sign

HELENA PATERSON

Illustrated by
Margaret Walty

1998
Llewellyn Publications
St. Paul, Minnesota 55164-0383, U.S.A.

The Celtic Lunar Zodiac © 1992, 1997 by Helena Paterson. All rights reserved. Printed in China. No part of this book may be used or reproduced in any manner whatsoever without written permission from Llewellyn Publications, except in the case of brief quotations embodied in critical articles and reviews.

Copyright © Illustrations 1992, 1997 Margaret Walty.

FIRST LLEWELLYN EDITION
Second Printing, 1998

Previously published in 1992 by Rider Books, London, England.

Cover Illustration: Margaret Walty
Chapter Illustrations: Margaret Walty
Cover Design: Lisa Novak
Book Typesetting: Peregrine Graphics Services
Project Management: Jan Feeney

Library of Congress Cataloging-in-Publication Data

Paterson, Helena, 1945–
      The Celtic Lunar Zodiac : how to interpret your moon sign / Helena
    Paterson : illustrated by Margaret Walty.--1st Llewellyn ed.
          p. cm.
      Includes bibliographical references.
      ISBN 1-56718-510-X (trade paper)
      1. Astrology. Celtic. 2. Moon--Miscellanea. 3. Zodiac.
      I. Title.
      BF1714.C44P383 1997
133.5'93916--dc21   97-5648
                                                                              CIP

Llewellyn Publications
A Division of Llewellyn Worldwide, Ltd.
P.O. Box 64383, St. Paul, MN 55164-0383

CONTENTS

To the Cailleach, the Old Veiled One.

I stood alone within the trees; alone I thought,

with all the world but rushing by, so lonely was I.

Who in this world could know my heart,

its aches, its hurts and striving to Thee? How lonely I was in Thee.

But as I stood there in the glade, a peace unknown went whispering by;

it looked at me a-standing there

and saw the heart in need of Thee, and stayed a

while.

from *A Reason for Living* by George Benton-Smith

ACKNOWLEDGMENTS

Thank you, James Vogh, for writing your book *Arachne Rising;* it inspired me to make a further study of the 13 Druidic signs by reading Robert Graves' masterly work on the subject, *The White Goddess.* Recognition must also be extended to the authors mentioned in the bibliography, whose contributions cannot be forgotten, only further praised.

Praise must also be attributed to Margaret Walty's magical interpretations—an artist of rare talent and imagination.

My grateful acknowledgments to the late Dr. John Penderill-Church and Edward Harte, two extraordinary characters who lived in Cornwall and who restored long-lost historical myths to their rightful place in the local archives. It was John's paper, titled "Herbs for the Use of Healers," given at the annual conference of the National Federation of Spiritual Healers in 1979 that provided the outline information on Druidic herbs.

Special thanks to the staff at Llewellyn—Nancy Mostad, Lynne Menturweck, Andrea Godwin, Jan Feeney, and Judy Gilats—whose helpful suggestions and editorial skills gave the whole content a sharper focus. Thanks are also due to J. L. White, astronomer, who advised on the astronomical data. Also to the many friends who loaned their precious books.

—Helena Paterson

INTRODUCTION

The Druids

The Druids, a Celtic priesthood who lived in the British Isles from around 1000 B.C., used a lunar calendar of 13 months, each consisting of 28 days, and one intercalary day, to calculate their year and their important festivals. The ritual aspect of their religion was based primarily on the soli/lunar cycle, their zodiac being lunar rather than solar. This reflects a culture based on matrilineal succession. The Druidic religion was drawn from a keen awareness of the natural and supernatural energies identified with the spirits *(dryads)* of their sacred trees, and the Druids' zodiac of tree spirits were emanations that they believed came to Earth from the Sun.

Many centuries later the medical knowledge of herbal medicine relating to the trees and plants of the Druids was found to be surviving in Ireland. Druidic medicine is thus chiefly known from the Irish records of *The Book of the O'Hickeys* and *The Book of the O'Lees,* both now preserved in the Royal Irish Academy. These books were written in 1303 and 1443 respectively, partly in Latin and partly in Irish, and probably represent the largest number of ancient medical manuscripts still in existence in any language.

The Druidic god of healing, Diancecht, whose name means "swift in power," has long been regarded as the fount of all Irish medical and herbal lore. But his son, Midoch, and daughter, Airmida,

apparently excelled him in the leech's art, and in a fit of jealousy Diancecht slew his son. However, from the grave of the young god sprang 365 herbs from the joints and sinews of the dead body, each possessing a magic virtue to heal the diseases of the related parts. In this respect Midoch resembles the young Aesculapius, Greek god of healing, who incurred the jealousy of Jupiter and was struck down with a thunderbolt. In Celtic myth, gods were sometimes personified as the calendar year; in the myth relating to Midoch he is thus honored, and remembered with the numerical life-giving symbol of the solar year and with a sacred herb representing each day.

In order to calculate any calendar or zodiac, a precise knowledge of the movement of the celestial bodies is required. Stonehenge, a source of many legends and a site of undiminished curiosity, has attracted scholarly studies for centuries. In recent years such study has yielded some profound information regarding the astronomical alignment of the ancient stones, showing that the solstices, equinoxes, and eclipses can all be accurately calculated, despite their variable declinations and complex cycles.

Although the Druids did not build Stonehenge, or any of the other Megalithic monuments in Britain and Ireland, it is perhaps a relevant observation that the Druidic religion only flourished where these ancient stones and burial chambers were located. The ancient Britons who had erected the imposing stone circles left a legacy shrouded in mystery and magic, with their own origins being as equally obscure as those of the Celtic invaders cast up from the sea. According to the archaeologists, very few hostilities resulted from the Celtic confrontation with the indigenous population, and it appears that an intermingling of tribal customs and cultures occurred over several centuries, long before the Roman invasion.

The Megalithic religion of the ancient British was based on what has been termed "the cult of the dead," and is almost identical to the Egyptian cult of Osiris, god of the dead, and the underworld. The Celtic people shared many aspects of their religion and culture with the Greeks, including a god of the underworld they called Dis, and from whom all Celts claimed descent. Dis resembles the Greek god Pluto, god of the underworld in Greek mythology, the most feared god, and, as Lord of the Infernal Regions, an initiator into their greater mysteries of life. This adds to the speculation about a common source or common ancestry between all four races—the ancient British, the Celts, the Greeks, and the Egyptians.

Druidic Astrology

Hidden in all astrology is the esoteric language of symbolism, which contains many references to source or origins. It is probable that within the astrology of the Druids lies the key to the origin of the Celts and possibly the ancient Britons, for the Druids had their own zodiac and cosmology that had obviously evolved in Britain around the stone circles and observatories of the Megalithic people. A summation of the Druidic religion, astrology, and mythology may also provide a more enlightened view of a race of people who have influenced the western world perhaps more conclusively than any other ancient people.

In the Druidic system of astrology the whole Earth was known as *Buarth Beirdd* or the bovine enclosure, and the Earth's fertility was symbolized by a white cow and the generating Sun by a white bull.

The circular half of the globe above the rational horizon was symbolized by the mystical Cauldron of Ceridwen (lunar goddess) that contained the divine feminine essence. It was further divided between the equinoctial line from east to west, with the Sun, Taliesin, having dominion over the half containing the longest day (summer solstice), and Avagddu or night ruling the other half containing the shortest day (winter solstice).

This primeval division of night and day was also basic to the Celtic conception of time—a dimension that had no boundaries, only entrances and exits. The astronomical markers located the portals where the emanations of divine life both entered and left Earth. The equinoxes and solstices were thus named: *Alban Eilir* (second generation) for the first vernal equinox; *Alban Hefin* (sunny temperature) for the summer solstice; *Alban Elfed* (harvest) for the autumnal equinox; and *Alban Arthuan* for the winter solstice (Arthur's season) when Arthur was engaged in fighting the powers of darkness. Reference to King Arthur in their cosmology came later, but it was a Celtic tradition to identify heroes and kings with the solar deity.

Druidic Religion

The Druidic religion has a higher philosophy and tradition that is seldom touched upon. The Druids believed in a creator who could not be seen by man, and whose own emanation was beyond comprehension even to the initiated. For that reason they named him Celi, which meant "concealing," and his consort was the lunar goddess Ceridwen or "aid." They did not worship the Sun, but identified it with the only begotten son of Ceridwen, born from the mystical union between Ceridwen and Celi.

The divinity of the Sun was part of the ancient Druidic trinity that had preceded Christianity. It symbolized the three rays or emanations of their great creator Celi, not from the Sun itself. These three "fertilizing" rays were symbolized by three golden apples, and identified with the triune word or *logos* of the creator, which held the secret of the universe in its very breath.

Celi and Ceridwen were regarded as incomprehensible spirits, Ceridwen being the originator of crude matter that began in an embryonic condition from across the ocean—the source of all life. This essence of life was feminine and passive in its nature, and every spring it was brought over the seas in a sacred boat shaped like a crescent Moon and propelled by Ceridwen. The Sun was "reborn" as a babe of Ceridwen on December 22 (winter solstice) as it once again began its ascent in the sky.

It was thought by the Druids that myriads of lives, quite apart from the physical existence, also emanated at the same time and were led by the Sun from the dimension of *Annwn,* an astral plane located in the Celtic underworld, into the outer world. This "life" or soul-force, which had initially been deposited by Ceridwen, had evolved through the animal creation up to human form, but it was without the spiritual inspiration of *Awen,* the reasoning faculty imparted directly from God.

There were three circles of spiritual evolution: the circle of *Abred;* the circle of *Gwynvyd;* and the circle of *Ceugant.* From *Annwn* life crawled into *Abred,* the circle of trial—the Earth-plane where the soul-force took physical form. This included humanity and all below it, and was a place where good and evil were in equal measure and influence. Man was free from all obligation, and every act was one of consent and choice. As man evolved, so did his *Awen* and a clearer vision of God. In this Druidic system of evolution the "free will" of mankind was given great emphasis and considered to be an important factor, unlike the Brahmin religion that this aspect of Druidism has been said to resemble.

These "teachings" come from the disputed volume of material known collectively as *Barddas,* and were documents that had been gathered from more ancient manuscripts by the Welsh bard Iolo Morganwg. But careful reading of the *Barddas* does reveal several distinctly Celtic persuasions, the "enigma of the Bards" being a good example. It forms two parts, in the question and answer routine of a riddle, the thought-provoking exercise so popular amongst Celts. It begins:

There is nothing truly hidden but what is not conceivable;
There is nothing not conceivable but what is immeasurable;
There is nothing immeasurable but God;
There is no God but that which is not conceivable;
There is nothing not conceivable but that which is truly hidden;
There is nothing truly hidden but God.

The solution begins:

What is not conceivable is the greatest of all, and the immeasurable of what is not in place;
God is the greatest of all, and the immeasurable of intelligence;

And there can be no existence to anything but from intelligence;
And the non-existence of all things comes from what is not in place.

These statements underline the deeper philosophy of the Druids, and appear to share common ground with the *Qabalah,* an ancient Hebraic system of mystical evolution, as well as with Brahmin teaching and many other ancient religions.

The Druids also considered it possible for man to evolve to *Gwynvyd* during his lifetime through his own volition or the memory of God. In other words the Celt was certainly much more a "free agent" than his eastern counterpart. The idea of "memory" has links with the Egyptian preoccupation with learning all the names of their gods in order to make their way safely to their idea of heaven.

But the circle of *Abred* was one in which all mankind must pass through during their various stages of existence before being qualified to enter the circle of felicity—*Gwynvyd,* a plane of the wholly developed spirit. The circle of *Ceugant* was occupied by God alone, but there also existed a polarity of darkness called *Cythraul* that God had subdued by uniting with it.

Creation Myths

Ceridwen's other son, Avagddu—Night—was her first-born in the older evolutionary myths of the Celts, and later became the dark twin to the Sun.

This duality of light and darkness continued through all creation of life in Celtic thought and tradition. There are many parallel creation myths to "darkness" preceding "light." Apart from the most well-known one in the Bible, there is also mention of Lilith, whose name means "night," who was the first wife of Adam. In the Talmud, Lilith quarreled with Adam, left him and was pursued by three angels who sought unsuccessfully to persuade her to return and become the mother of mankind. Later, however, her insane jealousy of Adam's new wife Eve caused her to return and take revenge by instigating Cain's fury against his brother Abel.

In the Celtic myth of Ceridwen it was three drops from her sacred cauldron that transformed Gwion from a mortal child into a solar deity known as the bardic-god Taliesin. The birth of Taliesin was resented by the great lunar goddess, who cast the newborn babe back into the ocean. Both the Sun and Earth were seen as life-giving deities, but Ceridwen was the primeval mother, the lunar goddess whose power, like Lilith's, retained the more mystical and darker aspect of the female.

In Druidic mysticism the eclipses were the spectacular and awesome phenomenon that occurred when Celi formed a mystical union with either the Moon or Earth—hence their keen observance of such events. A lunar eclipse may be seen over the complete hemisphere of the Earth, and can only take place at full Moon; the Earth casts its own shadow in space, so during the lunar eclipse it is the shadow of the Earth that slowly creeps across the face of the Moon. It may form either a total or partial eclipse, but the light of the Moon does not vanish entirely, due to the layer of atmosphere around the Earth that refracts a certain amount of sunlight. Solar eclipses are much more spectacular and occur when the Moon stands between the Sun and Earth at the time of the new Moon.

All eclipses were seen by the Druids as a primeval replay of the regenerating forces of the spiritual energies in the universe. In all ancient astrological records eclipses were initially considered "evil," but later they were regarded as more auspicious events that could be either good or bad; it depended on whose gain or loss they signified, and were mostly linked to national events. The study of the eclipse cycles also formed part of the *Saros* tables of the Chaldeans and Babylonians, which were lunar-based, and were later examined by Meton, an Athenian astronomer who "rediscovered" the lunation cycles.

Traces of Atlantis

Apart from the Sun and Moon there were several other celestial bodies closely observed by the Druids. These were the constellations of the Pleiades, Orion, and Auriga, as well as some of the chief stars in the northern sky, namely Arcturus, Castor, and Deneb. Arcturus lies close to the tail of the Great Bear constellation, which, with Orion, forms the two main direction finders or navigational aids for all travelers and astronomers.

The mythology relating to the Great Bear is

both vast and very ancient; for example, it was known as the Seven Rishis in Hindu records. Astronomically it marked the precession of the equinoxes, the duration of *Yuga* revolutions or great ages. In Egyptian mythology the Great Bear was known as the Mother of Time and was called the Living Word; it gave rise to the symbol of the ankh-cross that represents the "loop" shape of the constellation. In their Osirian rituals it marked a place in the heavens where the Sun was reborn in the northern sky. In the bardic riddle of Gwion there is mention of the constellation as another marker or direction finder, along with the *Corona Borealis,* in trying to locate the mysterious Castle of Arianrhod.

Orion, the hunter whose brilliant retinue includes Sirius, the brightest star in the whole sky, lies south on a winter evening in the northern hemisphere. Its distinctive shape also points out the chief Geminian star, Castor. The Great Bear lies north-east, with the bright star Deneb belonging to the constellation of Cygnus almost on the northern horizon. Capella, the chief star of Auriga, is almost directly overhead. Capella, after the Sun and Moon, was the most closely studied star in the northern sky to be observed by the Druids. It is not the brightest star in the sky, but the alignment with the other constellations does place it directly overhead during the winter months.

The ancient civilization of Atlantis has been written about and speculated on for centuries. Many mythologists and esoterics believe that after the Great Deluge had annihilated the Atlantean civilization, the survivors and outpost colonists were scattered worldwide. They were the "original" people of the sea, who became the founders of all classic civilizations. According to Donnelly, in his book *Atlantis,* Plato, who lived 400 years before Christ, recorded the history of Atlantis from his ancestor Solon, a great law-giver of Athens. Solon had visited Egypt 200 years previously and been initiated by the Egyptian priests into the occult mysteries of great antiquity. The priests had also reputedly shown him sacred objects relating to Atlantis that confirmed its historical existence.

The island of Atlantis was said by Plato to have existed more than 9,000 years prior to the time of Solon, and was described as a large island known as "the Continent of Atlantis." It was apparently a great and wonderful empire that ruled over several other smaller islands, the remnants of which are now known as the Canaries and the island of Madeira. Part of this empire also included areas of Libya, Egypt, and Europe as far as Tyrrhenia (Etruria, in what is now Italy). Its founder was Poseidon, a primeval sea-god, who had mated with an Earth-born maiden, Cleito, to produce the first Atlantean people. Poseidon's ten children with Cleito were five sets of twins, the first-born being Atlas, and all the descendents became known as "the people of the sea" because of their lineage from Poseidon.

The island of Atlantis was considered by Plato to be a veritable paradise or Garden of Eden, immensely fertile and teeming with every sort of wildlife and exotic flora. Hot springs and inland lakes divided the island into several zones, which were cleverly bridged to allow access to all parts, and canals were dug, with sluice gates to control the tidal flow of the larger lakes. Many fabulous sea-beasts abounded in these waters, especially dolphins, who were treated with the greatest respect, as Poseidon himself was believed to be intimately related to this sacred species.

The buildings and temples of Atlantis were constructed with great skill, and ornamental stones were intermingled with natural stones to delight the eye, these stones being mainly white, red, and black. The Atlanteans also covered the outer walls with a coating of brass, so the total effect was a dazzling reflected light that appeared to encompass the whole of the island. The chief temple was dedicated to Cleito and Poseidon, and remained inaccessible because of its high enclosure made of gold and silver with an ivory roof. The only people to worship or visit this most holy temple were the gods themselves.

If this were true, it reflects the Druidic belief in the third circle of spiritual evolution, Ceugant, where God alone existed. The name Ceugant closely resembles the English word cygnet (a young swan), being derived from old French *cygne,* which originated from Greek *kuinos.* In the ancient myths of the Irish Celts the children of Lir were turned into swans, and became a symbol of the radiant divinity of their ancient gods. In Greek myth the names of their gods and goddesses were remembered in the constellations that bear their names, Cygnus being identified with Jupiter, who visited Leda in the disguise of a swan.

But the constellation of Cygnus is now more commonly known as the Northern Cross; it contains an expanding supernova remnant known as the Cygnus Loop, and is also believed to contain a black hole in space. Black holes in space have recently captured the imagination of the public, and are attracting much attention from astronomers; they represent the great unknown, the primeval "darkness" in our universe.

It was the Sons of Night or Darkness in Atlantean myth who upset the balance of their once orderly society. At one time the powers of light and darkness were equal, and there co-existed two priesthoods known as the Sons of Light and the Sons of Night. But in some esoteric belief the Sons of Night apparently strayed off their narrow left-hand path and fell into the abyss, which in turn generated an upsurge of demonic forces who corrupted the Atlanteans into acts of great depravity. Poseidon returned after a long absence, and discovered the chaos of war, with terrible battles raging between the two priesthoods. Consequently their civilization was doomed in the esoteric sense; Poseidon, saddened and angry, struck the island with his three-pronged sceptre or trident and there followed a catastrophic earthquake that rent the whole continent apart and a volcanic explosion completely engulfed the island, which sank in one day. The symbol and awesome power of his three-pronged trident is remarkably similar to the three rays associated with the Druidic god, which also represented the three most powerful words that may never be pronounced less they destroy the universe.

According to Donnelly, another surviving fragment of Atlantis, apart from Madeira and the Canaries, is said to be the Azores; hot springs still abound there, and its climate is very temperate considering its position in the Atlantic Ocean. Geologists have confirmed that the Azores were once part of a large continent, and deep-sea soundings have located a huge shelf or ridge situated in the mid-Atlantic. This ridge is shown on nautical charts, and is aptly named Dolphin's Ridge.

Helena Blavatsky, probably one of the greatest authorities on the occult, was another advocate of Atlantis and the Atlantean "root race" civilization. In her book *The Secret Doctrine* she makes the observation that the one link with Atlantis that all her "descendants" maintained, despite their assimilated cultures and religions, was a memory of their homeland whose location was hidden in the starlore of astrology. She refers to the ancient Sinhalese, who claim descent from Atlantis and who mention in their earliest astrological records "A time when the summer tropical color passed through Pleiades, when Cor Leonis would be upon the equator, and when Leo was vertical to Ceylon at sunset, then would Taurus (Pleiades) be vertical to the island of Atlantis at noon."

The constellation of the Pleiades has been constantly monitored by numerous races, from the Australian Aborigines to the North American Indians. The rising of the Pleiades is aligned to the Heel Stone at Stonehenge, and its mythology intimately relates the Celts with the ancient Greeks. In *The White Goddess,* Robert Graves' comparative study of Greek and Celt, it is recalled in the account recorded by the historian Hecateus. It describes the inhabitants of the British Isles, who were known as the Hyperboreans, as being particularly friendly with the Athenians and the Delians from remote times; indeed, their chief priest, Abaris, had visited Greece to renew their "family" connection with the

Delians. The Hyperboreans were regarded as gifted harpists and poets, who sang hymns to their mutual Sun god Apollo in their magnificent temple (Stonehenge?) that had been built to honor his birthplace in their island. Apollo was said to visit the temple every nineteen years (great lunar year), to play the harp and dance every night from the vernal equinox until the rising of the Pleiades. In ancient esoteric astronomy, Latona, Apollo's mother, represents the whole Hyperborean continent and its race. She is symbolically identified with the polar region and night, for the Sun always "reappeared" in this part of the northern sky.

This certainly relates to the Druidic religion and cosmology. Is the star pattern mentioned earlier, with Capella being almost directly overhead, the "Druidic marker" that provides a correct compass bearing for the Pleiades, to then be aligned with Atlantis and the British Isles? The Pleiades is undoubtedly at the center of some universal intrigue, just as its chief star, Alcyone, was reckoned to be at the central point around which our universe of fixed stars revolve.

During the darkness of winter the Druids looked up at the sky and observed the astral light. The rising of the Pleiades may have other significance but, if the star pattern they observed had any relevance, then the Pleiades would be aligned to the Atlantic Ocean where Atlantis is now said to lie submerged—and they are. If the original "people of the sea" were indeed the Atlanteans, then the Celts must not only be their descendants but, by retaining the same title, were perhaps the last remnants of their priesthood. The lack of hostility from the "natives" is perhaps a significant indication that they finally met up with other descendants of their own race. Their claim of being descendants of Dis, an underworld god, is really a claim of their belief in the immortality of the soul.

The association of the constellation of Auriga with the riddle of Gwion in trying to locate the mysterious Castle of Arianrhod would be most relevant if a positive link with Atlantis is to be established. Arianrhod represents one of the deeper mysteries in Celtic myth. She was primarily a lunar goddess, but she was also known as a dawn goddess because of her "fleeting light" in the sky. This particular aspect or disappearance at dawn may very well be the "timing" aspect of the star alignment observed by the Druids, which adjusted or maintained the exact position of Atlantis on the western horizon.

Arianrhod had twin sons, a solar deity called Llew, whom she had rejected (just as Ceridwen denied her solar child Taliesin), and a sea deity named Dylan. While this is an obvious symbolic reference to the rivalry between the solar and lunar deities, it also confirms an ancient lineage or association with the sea through their lunar goddess.

Like other ancient gods, the gods of the Celts were often born as twins. This could explain the interest in Castor, the chief star of the constellation of Gemini and the astrological sign of the heavenly twins. It also represents the duality of life—light and darkness, the basic pivotal principle on which their religion was founded—and mirrors once again Atlantean concepts.

Lunar Symbolism and Mythology

Arianrhod symbolizes the mysterious and mystical aspects of Druidism, and the mythology relating to her children has much relevance when deciphering the origins of the Celts. The twin to Llew, Dylan, became a popular marine deity, but the father of these twins was a mystery because Arianrhod had claimed to be a virgin immediately before their birth. She refused to be questioned by the powerful magician and underworld god, Math, who had managed to trick her into stepping over a magic wand, which in turn had the effect of producing the sudden birth of the twins.

The secretive nature of Arianrhod is well researched in James Vogh's book *Arachne Rising,* where he identifies Arianrhod, the "Lady of the Silver Wheel," with the constellation Auriga, which means "charioteer." He then associates her with the Cretan spider goddesses Arachne and Ariadne. Both were associated with tree worship in the Crete-Minoan period, and with secret labyrinths and hanged gods. He also makes the interesting point that Arianrhod was a Celtic goddess who stood at both ends of the thread of life, and the quest to find her "castle" was the quest for immortality.

Celtic kings wore a brooch in the shape of a "wheel" to symbolize their belief in the immortality of the soul.

This quest is also associated with the Celtic voyages to the "other world," a place where their gods were said to live. The other world consisted of a number of fabulous islands that lay due west on any compass bearing. From the British Isles and southern Europe this certainly relates to the Atlantic Ocean, and is perhaps another fragment of memory linking the Celts to Atlantis.

The Druids' Zodiac

The conclusions drawn by Vogh from the corresponding mythology of the Celts with the ancient Minoan people is that Arachne presided over a 13-sign zodiac that corresponds with the Druidic tree calendar. He further explains that the Greeks eventually settled for a 12-sign zodiac, but had obviously at

Comparison of Druidic and Graeco-Roman Zodiacs

DRUIDIC SIGN	MONTH	GRAECO-ROMAN ZODIAC
BIRCH, *Beth*	December 24–January 20	Capricorn
ROWAN, *Luis*	January 21–February 17	Aquarius
ASH, *Nion*	February 18–March 17	Aquarius/Pisces
ALDER, *Fearn*	March 18–April 14	Pisces/Aries
WILLOW, *Saille*	April 15–May 12	Aries/Taurus
HAWTHORN, *Uath*	May 13–June 9	Taurus/Gemini
OAK, *Duir*	June 10–July 7	Gemini/Cancer
HOLLY, *Tinne*	July 8–August 4	Cancer/Leo
HAZEL, *Coll*	August 5–September 1	Leo/Virgo
VINE, *Muin*	September 2–September 29	Virgo/Libra
IVY, *Gort*	September 30–October 27	Libra/Scorpio
REED, *Ngetal*	October 28–November 24	Scorpio/Sagittarius
ELDER, *Ruis*	November 25–December 23	Sagittarius/Capricorn

one time considered 13 signs and then decided against it. Thirteen is not a "rational number" and, by being associated with the ancient lunar goddesses, it has, he concedes, perhaps too many powerful taboos.

But the Druids had obviously adopted it, and then adapted it to form the soli/lunar cycle of both their calendar and zodiac, which places the Moon at the spiritual center and the solar cycle as the regenerating force. The Druidic zodiac also has some interesting associations and similarities with other ancient civilizations. Another prehistoric 13-sign zodiac has been found in America near Hot Springs, Arkansas, while yet another has been located in Aus-tralia, where an aboriginal stone carving found on Depuch Island shows the Moon's position in a zodiac of 13 signs.

Therefore the Druidic zodiac is not unique and, for people who would argue that the Druids' 13-month calendar does not necessarily constitute a 13-sign zodiac nor is sufficiently authenticated, I would recommend they read Robert Graves' and James Vogh's books, and check all the relevant references on the Druidic religion in the National Library of Wales in Aberystwyth. The Library's main catalog and *Llyfryddiaeth Llenyddiaeth Gymraeg* (a bibliography of Welsh Literature) has a list of works on

The Druidic Signs and Their Archetypes

DRUIDIC SIGN		PLANET	ARCHETYPAL CHARACTER	SYMBOLS
Birch	☉	Sun	Taliesin, Bardic-god	The eagle or stag
Rowan	♅	Uranus	Brigantia	Green dragon
Ash	♆	Neptune	Lir, sea-god	The trident
Alder	♂	Mars	Bran or Arthur	The pentacle
Willow	☽	Moon	Morgan le Fay	The serpent
Hawthorn	⚷	Vulcan	Govannan, smith-god	The chalice
Oak	♃	Jupiter	Dagda	The golden wheel
Holly	⊕	Earth	Danu	Flaming spear
Hazel	☿	Mercury	Ogma	The rainbow fish
Vine	♀	Venus	Branwen or Guinevere	The swan
Ivy	⚳	Persephone	Arianrhod	The butterfly
Reed	♇	Pluto	Pwyll, head of Annwyn	The stone
Elder	♄	Saturn	Pryderi, son of Pwyll	The raven

the Druids, particularly under section (ii) *Crefydd a Mytholeg* numbered 203–247. The corresponding library in Dublin, Ireland, has many copies of ancient manuscripts, and reference material too numerous to list. However, two useful and enlightening works, *The Book of Leinster,* a twelfth-century manuscript that preserves the integrity of the Druidic priesthood, and Joyce's book on the *Social History of Ancient Ireland,* are recommended.

Mythology is a complex record to decipher, and I can only add that, as a practicing astrologer of many years standing, I found overwhelming evidence for the Celtic lunar zodiac of 13 signs. Druidic astrology should be restored to a place of honor along with all the other ancient astrologies. Britain and Ireland have two "cosmic" centers—Stonehenge and Newgrange—that have never been fully appreciated by either historians or modern astronomers.

The chart on page 20, comparing Druidic signs with the Graeco-Roman zodiac, provides a useful guide to the Celtic lunar chart shown on page 23. The 13 signs of the Celtic lunar zodiac are divided through the 360 degrees by 12 signs of 28 degrees, while the last sign, the thirteenth, is the elder or *ruis* and contains 24 degrees. The last sign, by being smaller than the rest, represents the contraction of winter in the symbolic sense of reduced sunlight.

The title *Celtic lunar zodiac* may sound confusing to practicing astrologers, who would expect to see a zodiac based soley on lunar cycles. But the title was carefully chosen to denote the different approach to the whole subject of "solar astrology." The lunar-orientated zodiac is perhaps another "irrational" equation of feminine logic that has always existed to counter the rigid thinking of men. But it is also drawn from a source much closer to home and delves into the national psyche on many levels.

The first sign of the Celtic lunar zodiac begins with the birch tree and is associated with the letter *beth* in the Celtic tree alphabet. *Beth is* also the first of thirteen consonants of the Celtic letters that formed a calendar of seasonal tree magic. The Celts believed the spoken word had great power, the pitch or tone being harmful or harmonious, a curse or a poem. This is further explained in Chapter 9 of this book, where the power of the spoken word is related to the month of Coll, the sign of the hazel tree.

Archetypes are important sources of mythological and astrological interpretation, and their symbolism provides esoteric wisdom. In the chart on page 21 the Druidic tree signs are shown with their corresponding archetypal Celtic gods or mythical characters, and the associated ancient symbols, while the list of planetary rulers will provide relevant insight for astrologers.

There are also many mythical beings and relevant Celtic festivals associated with the signs, which have contributed to the interpretation in the following chapters. The significant line of poetry that introduces each sign has been drawn from the ancient Druidic incantation "The Song of Amergin," as revised by Robert Graves in his book *The White Goddess.*

There is a "missing" day in the Druidic calendar, the one intercalary day of December 23. It has been included under the sign of the elder, but it has a separate interpretation in Chapter 13. The significance of this "hidden" sign holds the key to the Dark Queen aspect of the lunar goddess Arianrhod. It is the essence of feminine wisdom that always remained concealed. People born on this "nameless day" have a cosmic spiritual awareness—time travelers akin to the Australian Aborigines whose dreamtime reflects an evolving creation and creator.

The flower and gemstone associated with each sign has been carefully selected to correspond and harmonize with the energies associated with the tree sign. The gemstones were also chosen from a range of precious and semiprecious stones used by the Druids as talismans for healing and protection.

The astrological chart shown on page 23 has been devised and drawn to equate the Celtic lunar chart with the Graeco-Roman chart. For all practicing astrologers it is still possible to draw up a natal chart and position the planets in the normal manner. For example, under the sign of the holly tree, the planet Earth may be substituted by Venus and the Moon substituted for Persephone, ruler of the ivy sign. Vulcan's orbit remains within the orbit of Mercury, and can be calculated from the tables by L. H. Weston.

The 13 signs "exist" within the 12-sign zodiac or the same 360 degrees—as they have always existed—and represent the "shadow zodiac" or yin principle. The ancient Chinese yin and yang concept represents two complementary energies whose interaction is thought to maintain the harmony of the universe and to influence everything within it. Yin is darkness, the feminine principle, and is symbolized by the Moon. Yang is brightness, the masculine principle, and is symbolized by the Sun.

The Celtic lunar chart will also add another dimension of interpretation by marking the symbolic ascent and descent of the Sun. This remains a "fixed" position, like a nautical compass-bearing, and relates to the heliocentric position of the Sun. The Druidic circles of spiritual evolution provide some interesting points relating to the exits and entrances of the solstices and equinoxes, and appear to mark some sensitive areas in the natal chart. The chart follows the geocentric movement of the planets used by most astrologers, but a future heliocentric interpretation may provide some highly original data. I am undertaking further study of the planetary positions through the Celtic tree signs, with a future book in mind.

The superb artwork that opens each chapter is by Margaret Walty. It provides a sense of fantasy and wondrous imagery, and the thirteen original portraits of character have all been meticulously researched to provide an authentic vision of the magical qualities within us all, often lying forgotten or inert, cast aside by the pace of modern life. For people who have never felt at ease with or been convinced by their traditional Sun sign, the Celtic lunar zodiac may provide an alternative guide.

THE CELTIC
LUNAR CHART

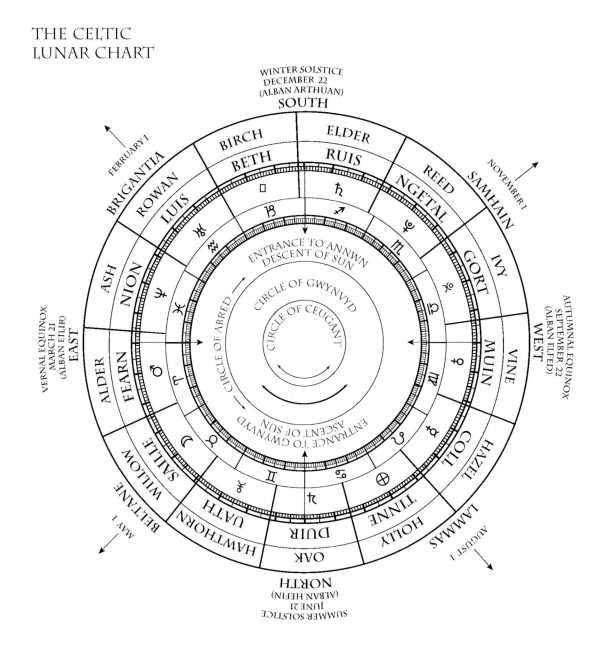

WINTER SOLSTICE
DECEMBER 22
(ALBAN ARTHUAN)
SOUTH

VERNAL EQUINOX
MARCH 21
(ALBAN EILIR)
EAST

AUTUMNAL EQUINOX
SEPTEMBER 22
(ALBAN ELFED)
WEST

NORTH
(ALBAN HEFIN)
JUNE 21
SUMMER SOLSTICE

FEBRUARY 1

NOVEMBER 1

MAY 1

AUGUST 1

BRIGANTIA

SAMHAIN

BELTANE

LAMMAS

BIRCH
BETH

ELDER
RUIS

ROWAN
LUIS

REED
NGETAL

ASH
NION

IVY
GORT

ALDER
FEARN

VINE
MUIN

WILLOW
SAILLE

HAZEL
COLL

HAWTHORN
UATH

HOLLY
TINNE

OAK
DUIR

ENTRANCE TO ANNWN
DESCENT OF SUN

CIRCLE OF GWYNVYD

CIRCLE OF CEUGANT

CIRCLE OF ABRED

ENTRANCE TO GWYNVYD
ASCENT OF SUN

The Signs

CHAPTER ONE
THE BIRCH TREE

BETH

December 24 – January 20

Symbolizing: The Sun
Gemstone: Rock crystal
Flower: Daisy
Archetypal Character: Taliesin, bardic-god

"I am a stag of seven tines"

The Illustration

The stark beauty of the birch in winter symbolizes the serenity of nature dormant and sleeping. The spirit of the birch tree projects a faint aura of light, as the Sun, representing the solar-king, begins to rise from the dark slumber of night. The tree is shown in the ethereal light to symbolize the divinity of the *dryad* or tree spirit. The golden eagle circles overhead, carrying in his sharp talons a salmon, a dazzling symbol of knowledge. The proud white stag is a symbol of the eventual fate of the Sun-king, who will reign for seven months in the 13-month lunar calendar of the Druids. This was foretold by the chief bard in the "Song of Amergin," an epic poem chanted as an incantation to establish their supremacy when the Celts first set foot on Irish soil. The daisy represents another ancient Celtic symbol of light.

The Rock Crystal

This is a naturally occurring substance that has the ability to make invisible light visible by refraction. The alchemists and magicians of medieval Europe claimed that if it was cut in a certain way and exposed to the Sun, it could also render a solid object invisible. It is a transformer of energy that relates to inception, the spiritual significance of the birch tree.

The Druids reputedly used rock crystal to make themselves invisible and thus be able to travel great distances undetected. The tribal aborigines of Australia continue to use amulets as a protection against demons, and the most commonly used stones for this purpose are fragments of rock crystal.

If held in both hands, rock crystal is said to induce serenity, a peace of mind, and to sharpen the mental processes.

The Stag

From ancient times the stag was considered a royal beast, and figured prominently in Celtic myths and legends. Antlers have been found in the Newgrange burial site in Ireland, and in various sites around Britain, notably at Stonehenge and Glastonbury. A stag cult appears to have first developed among the Gaulish Celts and then spread to Britain, being particularly active around Glastonbury. The horned deity called Cernunnos became an important intermediary between the animal kingdom, the forces of nature and man. It was a guardian of the gateway connecting a dual world envisaged by the Celts.

The fate of the antlered king, like the proud white stag, had an inevitable conclusion; both were symbols of the metamorphic process of soul growth that required radical changes on all levels of consciousness. The Celts drew heavily on their observations of nature in order to understand their own doubts and fears of life and death.

The Golden Eagle

This was another symbol of the soul, signifying the eventual resurrection, the power of life over death. As a bird of prey, the prize of knowledge symbolizes its ultimate victory.

The golden eagle is now almost extinct in

Britain; it is a powerful bird of magnificent flight, but seldom seen except in the north of Scotland. Highland chieftains still wear three golden-eagle feathers in their bonnets to proclaim their rank.

In heraldry the eagle is a bird that makes the most prominent appearance, although it is surprisingly lacking in English devices and coats of arms; the English imagination is perhaps not so wild or free in spirit as that of the Celt. It was used as a heraldic device by the Earls of Cornwall, who occupied a very Celtic kingdom, and some of whom had Celtic Origins.

The Romans used the golden eagle extensively on their standards and great seals. The French from Charlemagne to Napoleon used it with superb style and artistry. The Austrians adopted it early on, but developed it into a double-headed black emblem that was annexed by Germany. Black birds, however, have always had a sinister association, both symbolically and esoterically; the Austrian royal family, along with several other royal houses in Europe, incorporated the black eagle in their coat of arms, but most of these families have been either deposed or the royal heirs tragically eliminated. Coincidental or not, black eagles have a powerful occult significance that could never be termed benevolent.

The Druids were believed to be able to change into the form of all birds and beasts, their favorite being the eagle. The very idea of shape-changing is difficult for modern man to accept, but metaphysical studies relating to the rapid changes of molecular structure do not rule out such a phenomenon. The Druids had perhaps tapped into energies that are still waiting to be explored and understood by modern man.

The Common Daisy

This is a symbol of innocence and fidelity. Devotion to duty and personal obligation also describe the most positive aspects of the birch tree character. The daisy has an ancient lineage whose botanical name, *Bellis perennis,* came originally from a *dryad* called Belidis according to some writers of antiquities. It can be further traced to Belenos, a Celtic god of light and a solar deity.

The healing power of the daisy and yarrow was used by Druids on the battlefields with great effect; yarrow was used to staunch the bleeding, while the daisy was a great wound healer that counteracted the debilitating shock of such injuries. Both plants grow profusely over wide areas, but only the daisy grows all year round and throughout the world—an evergreen of plant power that complements the durability of the birch.

The Birch Tree

The birch tree is a native of Europe, from Sicily to Iceland, and parts of northern Asia, where it has been referred to as the Lady of the Woods for its grace and beauty. However, despite its slender beauty, it is hardier than the oak and will thrive in places where the sturdy oak will die. It was also used for many humble purposes, from providing broom handles to the manufacture of cloth. The name of the birch is a very ancient one, probably derived from the Sanskrit word *bhurga*. It is known as a tree whose bark is used for writing upon. The birch tree is associated with the letter *beth* in the Celtic tree alphabet, the first of the thirteen consanants of the Celtic letters that formed a

calendar of seasonal tree magic. In heraldry, the birch tree forms part of the Birkin family arms.

During the first lunar month of the year, the Celts used birch rods in the beating of the bounds and in driving out the spirit of the old year—two important rituals of re-establishing tribal boundaries and the order of the seasons. In Great Britain and Ireland birch rods were later used for flogging criminals, a practice continued right up to the present century and only recently rescinded in the Isle of Man. (Although part of the British Kingdom, the Isle of Man is an ancient Celtic stronghold with its own parliament, the Court of Tynwald.) Then in March the Druids made incisions in the tree and collected the sugary sap to make a cordial to celebrate the vernal equinox. It was also a very symbolic gesture of releasing the spirit *(dryad)* of the tree at the time of the Sun's own liberation into manhood. Indeed, in the Druidic herbal calendar the birch tree had a continuous cycle of uses throughout the year, with every part of the tree yielding a valuable remedy or product. While their observation of the rhythmic laws of nature was fundamental to their

social customs and agricultural calendar, spiritually the birch was the alpha and omega, the first and last principle, signifying the eternity of God and immortality of the soul.

Beth

Beth is a word strikingly similar to *Bith* (meaning world), the son of Noah and father of Cessair who, with the pilot Ladra, were the first people to invade or settle in Ireland according to the Irish *Mythological Cycle of Invasions.* They came to Ireland from the west, after a great deluge had overwhelmed the Earth. The shadow of Atlantis falls across this period of history, providing another mysterious connection relating to the Celts.

According to another earlier but lost ancient manuscript, *The Book of Druim Snechta,* the name of the first woman who settled in Ireland before the Flood was Banba, a female progenitor who symbolized both water and land in the creation myth of the ancient Irish.

The Solar Symbolism

The solar symbolism associated with the tree is a sign of the continuous phases of life, which aligns very well with the alpha-omega principle. The Sun, in terms of Celtic mythology, was a powerful deity. It was a cosmic allegory of Druidic belief, and had been created by the mystical union of Celi and

Ceridwen. The Welsh bards called this offspring Taliesin, and recounted his solar brilliance in the romantic and intellectual deeds of numerous poems.

The Irish and Gaulish Celts, a more warlike people, called their Sun-king Lugh and they regarded him as the greatest of warriors. He had an equally

mysterious birth as Taliesin, and a strange fostered upbringing with the Dark King of the Great Plain in the land of the living and the dead—a faery kingdom. He was therefore very skilled in all the secret arts and sciences. He had many titles, but as Lugh Lamfada, or Lugh of the Long Arm, he was guardian of a magical sword and spear, the two symbols of power and mastery over other races in battle. The other two symbols, the Lia Fail or Stone of Destiny and the Cauldron of Dagda, enabled the Celtic kings to believe in rule by divine right and to understand the deepest mysteries of life.

The Celts were naturally drawn to delving into the subterranean structures of life, both spiritually and philosophically, perhaps because they believed that all Celts were descendants of Dis, a powerful god of the underworld. Pluto, lord of Hades, was the Greek equivalent, the Greeks being a race with whom the Celts shared many beliefs and customs.

The Sun-king belief gradually evolved as the Celts experienced the changing eons of time. The sacrificial aspect became identified with Jesus, which certainly helped to promote their early conversion to Christianity. The solar spirit was equated with the national psyche, not only ready to be drawn into action at the time of approaching danger but also a guardian of national honor and truth. Just as Lugh went to the aid of the men of Ulster in their desperate hour of need, King Arthur personified Celtic chivalry. This solar spirit lies deep within the psyche of birch tree characters, and holds the key to unlocking their innermost feelings.

Myths Associated with the Sign

The story of the birth of Taliesin provides a glimpse into the Celtic world of fantasy and fundamental truths. Ceridwen was an ancient lunar goddess and a primeval mother figure. Her first-born child was called Avagddu, Black Wings, and in their creation myth was referred to as Night or Chaos. Avagddu was so ugly that Ceridwen decided to compensate him with the gift of great wisdom and knowledge. She prepared a mystical cauldron of inspiration to be filled with the sacred herbs of every species, their optimum virtues determined by the hours or position of the Moon and planets. It would take a year and a day to brew (a reference to the lunar calendar),

during which time she traveled far and wide to collect the ingredients.

In her absence, the task of stirring the cauldron was given to Gwion, son of Gwreany, the Herald of Llanfair. But on the day it was ready, three drops flew out, scalding his finger, which he quickly stuck in his mouth. In an instant he was transformed from a boy to man, student to sage. Realizing at once that the whole essence of the brew was contained in those three drops and that the residue was now a deadly poison, he fled, knowing full well the fury of Ceridwen. He used his new knowledge to change into the elements, then into a hare, a fish, a bird; but

Ceridwen pursued him as a greyhound, an otter, and a hawk. Finally, in desperation, he took the form of a grain of wheat, hiding amongst the many thousands on a threshing floor. But the goddess of all life was not so easily deceived. Turning herself into a large black hen, she gobbled him up. He grew inside her, however, and was born nine months later as her second son. Angry as she was for bearing a child of such trickery, she could not kill him because of his radiant beauty; instead, she concealed him in a leather bag, placed the bag in a coracle, and cast him unto the mercy of the sea. He was found and fostered (a typical Celtic concept of how man evolved from contact with the gods), and grew up to become the master bard Taliesin, who raised the skills of Welsh bardism to new heights and recognition.

This feat of great achievement, against all the odds, reveals a vein of optimism and enterprise running deep within the Celtic psyche. It also expresses their belief in the free spirit of man, which cannot be easily snuffed out or compromised—a complete contrast to eastern mysticism that demands a more obedient spiritual will.

Astrological Significance

The significance of the Sun in traditional astrology is simply "the life-giver," a vital and principal influence throughout the whole birth chart. Its position reveals the individual faculties. The symbol itself, a circle with a small dot in the center, represents the one unity underlying all things. Until a certain stage of evolution has been reached it therefore represents the self or the ego. Esoteric astrology defines the Sun on another level altogether; the Sun is observed as a focus of a ray from the central Sun or the supreme intelligence, presiding over the whole universe.

The 12-sign zodiac that has dominated western astrology for centuries has tended to interpret the Sun through the signs in a rather isolated or abstract way. The Sun in this system is regarded as the ruler of Leo, a fire sign that supposedly dominates other signs. But the soli/lunar cycle of the Druids provides a balance of energies, placing the Sun at the beginning of the Celtic zodiac, a place where it begins its return or "rebirth" after reaching the maximum point of declination or distance from Earth in the northern hemisphere. This new rulership sets a new precedent in astrological thinking, which will hopefully help to refocus and redefine the role of the Sun.

Archetypal Character

The mystical legend of Taliesin relates to the basic personal qualities associated with the birch tree sign, and reveals the individual facets of character. Taliesin is the archetypal birch tree character, symbolizing the potential light of the Sun, although any achievement or personal recognition has to follow a similar course or ordeal experienced by Taliesin. Therefore the basic character is primarily molded and influenced by the need for patience, which naturally evokes an inward sense of quiet determination as well as a sense of personal isolation.

There is, however, a basic inflexibility in this sign, symbolized by the changing forms of Gwion as he seeks to escape from the goddess. The eventual outcome is the radiant "rebirth" of the higher self in the form of Taliesin. In personal terms the birch tree character must learn to become less narrow-minded and rigid regarding all aspects of life.

Tree Character

Birch tree characters hold the seed potential of all the signs. The virtue of patience is attributed to this sign, a necessary requirement when dealing with such potential. People born under this sign direct their energy and enterprise through ambitious strategy; each step taken in life has a specific goal in mind. The obstacles can, however, be quite formidable. Personal limitations are not readily accepted, as birch tree characters become more resolute and determined. Some notable birch tree characters include Louis Pasteur, Johannes Kepler, William Ewart Gladstone, and Lloyd George.

Positive Aspects

Birch tree characters are reliable and trustworthy people, not given to rash moves or bold statements. The second-son aspect in the mythology of the sign has an interesting parallel, pyschologically speaking. Birch tree characters often take on the role of head of the house, not through seniority of birth, but because they take family responsibilities very seriously. They are usually the most successful members of the family in financial terms, although they might not appear so as they do not flaunt their success or generally waste money on the symbols of affluence.

Negative Aspects

A rigid outlook can promote a pessimistic character and impose a form of self-discipline that can be difficult to sustain. Their willpower can therefore alternate, or fall between two extremes, resulting in some wild behavior or acting out of character that may surprise even close colleagues. It may, however, go to the other extreme of acting with great discipline and determination at certain times—but never consistently. Undisciplined birch tree characters are unhappy individuals.

General

Birch tree characters actually thrive best on strict routines and regimes. The term "workaholic" fits them perfectly, although it can equally apply to other signs, particularly other cardinal signs.

The best way to understand this tendency is to look again at the ambitious strategy; work is the means to an end, but do they really enjoy being the only person left in che office at the end of the day? It may be a question all birch tree characters should ask of themselves every so often, in order to define their true objectives in life. The intense desire to succeed is the bottom line and, on balance, is a positive aspect overall. The formidable obstacles mentioned earlier usually arise from difficult family obligations or physical weaknesses, all relating to setbacks from childhood; personal isolation has occurred at some stage, which is difficult to admit to or confront, and yet it has helped to strengthen some minor weaknesses of character.

Are birch tree characters sociable? Their quiet reserve can be deceptive. Providing they can choose the company, which falls into a narrow list of possibles rather than probables, they are certainly more amenable. After all, socializing is a serious matter if you are intent on becoming the managing director or, perhaps, marrying the managing director.

The trouble is, they are serious individuals trying not to be serious. If you should meet one who acts just the opposite, beware! They have an identity problem. But with regard to neuroses or phobias, these people are the least likely to be affected; both physically and mentally, they have developed a powerful resistance to just about everything. Having said that, they can become obsessive about their health, in the sense of sticking to a fairly strict regime; certain foods may be religiously avoided, and this establishes a mode of living that is, again, a necessary discipline.

Do birch tree characters have a sense of humor? They could never be termed humorous people, but their sense of humour has a droll quality that can have some people rolling in the aisles. But what makes them laugh is another matter. It would have to be extremely clever witticisms or jokes so coarse as to make most people blush. The extreme is the norm because mediocrity is not acceptable in their system of values.

With regard to material values, the birch tree characters have no problems whatsoever. They, above all other signs, understand the value of money; not only have they worked hard to acquire it, they are not ashamed or embarrassed about having it.

Do birch tree characters make good friends? The answer is undoubtedly yes, but not many people will get close enough to count themselves as such. They do make very good bosses, not overly generous with praise, but at the end of the day they will make sure that their employees have been fairly treated, and they are keen to promote people from humble origins. There is an autocratic manner that some people may find cold or indifferent. Although this quality is genuine enough, and related to an inherent sense of dignity, it is also a good cover-up for a basic shyness. Of all the signs, the birch tree character is also the most modest individual.

Love Life

There is an initial sense of loneliness associated with this sign that reflects a lack of activity or sensitivity regarding early personal relationships.

Successful marriages will often occur later in life and, along with holly tree characters, people born under this sign are not inclined to divorce. Separations are more likely, or the premature death of spouses. Their love life is rather hit and miss—some sudden passionate affairs, and then zilch. It has to fit into that strict routine, which, no matter how pleasurable, has a narrow circuit

Summary

Some of these points of character may not be so positive or pronounced, but the potential pattern is always there. Not all birch tree characters will come from the same family background, or have the same natural abilities, but there is a distinct behavior pattern that separates them from the rest of the crowd and applies throughout the zodiac.

Birch tree characters prefer to keep a low profile generally. Even if they attain high office or public standing, they prefer their private life to be very private. Their public image is often a matter of convenience to fit the part. Their careers remain a dominant influence overall, and there is no mistaking their personal hand on the wheel. They set their own precedents, and eventually create a degree of growth or success not easily matched by other signs of the zodiac.

CHAPTER TWO

THE ROWAN TREE

LUIS

January 21 – February 17

Symbolizing: *The planet Uranus*
Gemstone: *Peridot*
Flower: *Snowdrop*
Archetypal Character: *Brigantia*

"I am a wide flood on a plain"

The Illustration

The rowan tree is a magical tree, known as the tree of life in Celtic legend, and guarded by a fiery green dragon—a powerful symbol of life at a time of the year when night still rules the day. The dominance of the Moon is portrayed by the lunar spirit in the form of the snowdrop, a sign of consolation.

The tree stands in the sacred center of Stonehenge, ancient gathering place long before the Celts arrived in Britain. The feathery greenery and dense clusters of fire-red berries paint a vibrant splash of color in the gray world of winter. Stonehenge symbolically formed a huge candle at the Celtic feast of Candlemas, which marked the quickening of the year. The silver shafts of light of the Moon intermingle with the red glow of the faint light of the candles—the symbolic germination process attributed to the Celtic goddess Brigantia, who presided over the mystical aspect of the fertilization of the cold Earth. The fiery breath of the dragon ignited the vital current of energy that permeates the stones, symbolically regenerating the flame of eternal life.

The Peridot Stone

This is one of the oldest known stones. It is a pale green variety of the olivine chrysolite, a plutonic igneous rock derived from magma or lava that has solidified on or below the Earth's surface—a metamorphic substance relating to fire, the ancient symbol of light.

It was once regarded as the most powerful magic stone by all ancient people. The Egyptians and Babylonians used it extensively in amulets as a protection against the evil eye and witchcraft. The ancient Greeks made a headband of the stones, which enabled the wearer to foretell the future and speak with spirits. The Druids also stitched these stones, among others, into their robes, for protection and to strengthen the mind.

Dragons

In world myths dragons represent the supernatural forces that usually guard great secrets and treasures. In Celtic mythology the dragon is a fiery winged serpent associated with the serpent cult of the Druids, a branch of Druidism connected with magical rites relating to alchemy and the mysterious energies of ley lines.

Merlin, the arch-Druid of Celtic mysticism, who is still something of a personal enigma, gave warnings and prophecies concerning dragons. He warned King Vortigern, a Christian Celt, not to build a defensive tower against the pagan Saxons because it would disturb the two sleeping dragons who lay beneath the site in a dark mere. One dragon was red and the other white, a potent formula of alchemy, representing the positive and negative energies dormant in all creation. Furthermore the red dragon represented the British Celts and the white dragon the Saxons. Vortigern, a treacherous monarch, was eventually killed by his own people for inviting the Saxons over to Britain as allies against their old enemies, the Picts and Vikings. The disastrous consequence of this alliance was that the Saxons then decided to stay and make their own bid for power.

The analogy of prematurely upsetting or activating the dormant energies of the dragons has deep implications, in this instance relating to the future confrontations of the Celts and Saxons.

The red dragon (positive energy) became the emblem of Wales and of the future dynasty of the Tudors, an illustrious family who spawned great monarchs during crucial periods of history in Britain. Prior to the rise of the Tudors, the War of the Roses (late fifteenth century) was fought by the Lancastrians and Yorkists for control of the English throne, the eventual winners being the Lancastrians, whose emblem was the red rose. The act of conjoining the two roses, one red, one white, by the ultimate victor, Henry Tudor, had more subtlety than was perhaps obvious. However, Henry was not only observing the importance of symbolism, but was also fulfilling the ancient prophecy of Merlin, who had foreseen such a union. While in prison during this period, Sir Thomas Malory, a Yorkist knight, had written the greatest literary work of the century, *Morte d'Arthur,* as a tribute to Celtic chivalry. This was significant timing considering Henry's Welsh ancestry—a powerful Celtic bloodline—and indicates a change of loyalties on Malory's part. Malory, who had been imprisoned on the charges of theft, extortion, rape, and attempted murder, seems a most unlikely advocate of chivalry, and remains a rather shadowy figure in history.

But it was this union of the Celt and Saxon that transformed two distinctly different races into a mighty nation. The cultural aspects remained separate, but their united strength became a formidable challenge and defense against all opposing forces. It is perhaps interesting to note that, since this union, the only invading forces to succeed were the Norman French, who came from a similar mixture of Gaul and Viking.

The name Pendragon belonged to another illustrious and more ancient Celtic lineage, that of King Arthur of Camelot and the Holy Grail legend. His name of Pendragon translates as "head" or "chief-dragon." His father, Uther Pendragon, had derived his name from a mysterious comet that resembled two golden dragons. It suggests a mystical lineage with powerful supernatural affiliations. The whole saga of Arthur, from birth to his strange disappearance at death, has an uncanny quality that doesn't quite relate to previous myths of Celtic kings and gods.

Candlemas

Candlemas was a Celtic Christian festival celebrated on February 2. According to Arthurian legend, it was the time when the Celtic barons gathered around the stone holding the sword that would proclaim their rightful king. Arthur Pendragon was thus armed with a symbol of divine right at a time when the penetrating light of the Sun was beginning to pierce the night of Avagddu. This association with the power of the Sun is a parable with Uranus, the power of vision or progressive thinking holding the key to man's own divinity. The true source, however, goes even further back in Celtic memory.

Candlemas was also the Christianized version of an ancient festival of candles in honor of Brigit or Brigantia, a triune Moon goddess. The Virgin Mary was duly substituted for Brigantia, and the sacred flame rekindled from the festival of Brigantia, a Celtic spring festival in her honor. Brigantia,

Beltane, Lammas, and Samhain were the four fire-festivals marking the spiritual beginnings of the seasons. Candlemas or Brigantia was seen as the rebirth of spirit, the spiraling out again from darkness.

Brigantia

This name is derived from Brighid or Brigid, a most powerful Celtic goddess. She was the power of the new Moon, of the spring of the year and of the flowing sea. In Ireland she was most revered, and in Britain she was the goddess of the Brigantes, a widespread tribe. Each year, as the first glimmer of dawn appeared, the Cailleach, representing the old-woman aspect of their triune goddess, was transformed into the fair young goddess bride.

Her festival was also called Oimelc, and the rites were celebrated with elaborate preparation by the married women of the tribe. They smeared their bodies with woad and marched naked to the ceremony as a mark of respect to the departure of Cailleach, the Old Veiled One, while the younger members of the tribe collected food and money to make offerings at the shrine of Brigid. The ceremonies took place at such shrines; just as the holy shrine in Mecca draws Moslems from around the world, so Stonehenge was the open-air cathedral where the Celts also reverently gathered, if only once in their lifetime.

Stonehenge

Stonehenge relates to the remote past, but retains a mysterious aura to this present day. The original builders may not have been Celtic, but the Druids certainly used the site for the purpose intended. This was primarily for astronomical observations, for, whatever else has been associated with this great Megalithic site, no one can deny that the exact alignment of the stones provides a precise soli/lunar observatory. And whatever else was conducted there—burials or ritual sacrifices, for example—is open to conjecture.

The Druidic religious and social calendar mentioned previously was ceremoniously orchestrated by this cycle. The fire-festivals and solstices relied on the precise calculations of the two great luminaries and the ability of the Druids to predict them. The history of the construction of Stonehenge followed three phases, starting sometime around 3200 B.C., with the final phase occurring around 2600 B.C. During this 600-year period Stonehenge evolved from a simple but imposing earthwork enclosure with one standing stone to the magnificent towering circle of Sarsen stones encapsulating the fabulous bluestones. The trilithon design of two stones supporting a third crosspiece lintel to form a complete circle is unique to Stonehenge and not found in other Megalithic sites or any other ancient stone buildings. The uniqueness of Stonehenge poses many unanswerable questions, but the people who utilized its position and awesome majesty were the Celts.

The Snowdrop

This is the first wild flower of the year, and has been referred to as the Candlemas bell, confirming its association with the festival, but it is not a native plant to Britain. According to old herbals, the monks brought the tiny bulbs of the plant with them from Italy during the medieval period. They called it the bulbous violet, and used it as a wound healer and for digestive problems. It quickly became naturalized and spread in considerable masses around the countryside. It is a dainty little flower that complements the graceful beauty of the rowan.

The Rowan

The rowan tree or mountain ash is closely related to the rose, and is a cousin of the hawthorn, the apple, and the pear. It is not, however, related to the true ashes, having derived its name from the similarity of the leaves. It has also been called the "whispering tree" because, in some ancient legends, it had secrets to tell those who would listen. It is seen at its best among the wild glens in the north and west of Scotland, where it is known as the "lady of the mountains."

Sprigs of rowan are the clan badges of three Highland clans—Menzies, Malcolm, and Maclachlan. All have historic associations with the Scottish crown, but the Maclachlans have the most ancient lineage, dating back to Robert the Bruce. Their clan chief was killed at Culloden, and his horse made the long journey alone back home to Strathlaclan, but no one could catch him. The horse, covered in the blood of his master, galloped around the castle once and disappeared into the descending mist of the mountains. According to Highland legend, he appears from time to time as a ghostly specter and, if anyone is close enough to hear his sad whinny, then tragedy will strike the family. The rowan has always been associated with protection against witchcraft and bad luck, which is perhaps why the Maclachlans pinned it on their bonnets.

The Celts also believed that no witches or evil spirits could cross a door over which a branch of rowan had been nailed. It was planted around dwellings and in lonely places to act as a deterrent against evil spirits and the awesome force of lightning. In Wales it was once planted in every churchyard to scare away the demons who might disturb the sleep of the dead.

During the second lunar month the Druids made rowan wattles, consisting of a frame of rods tied with leather thongs made from bulls' hides, which were used to compel demons to answer difficult questions in order to divine the future. Bewitched horses and animals were also controlled by rowan wands and whips at a time when the sky was full of omens and a strange new light; lightning was prone to strike suddenly and storms raged across the land and sea. At this restless time in Celtic Ireland, rowan stakes were driven through corpses to immobilize their ghosts; rowan fires were kindled by the Druids, over which incantations were spoken to summon spirits to take part in forthcoming battles; and the magical power of the rowan was used throughout the year to combat all evil forces.

The fruit and the bark of the rowan have medicinal powers—there are many old recipes and remedies made from the rowan tree. It was used by the Druids as a gargle for sore throats, and later in the year the fruit made a delicious jelly to eat with game. The Welsh made a special ale brewed from the berries, while the astringent properties found in all parts of the tree were used in tanning and making the black dye used for Druidic robes; white robes were the ceremonial robes worn by Druids, but black robes were also worn at certain lunar ceremonies—the waning part of the lunar cycle, and the eclipses. The Druids of Anglesey, who confronted the Romans in a desperate attempt to throw back the might of Rome, attired themselves in black in order to perform their darker rites, evoking demonic forces.

Luis

The connection of the rowan tree or *luis* with Candlemas is shown by Morann MacMain's Ogham in the *Book of Ballymote,* where he gives the poetic name of the rowan as "delight of the eye," from *lui-siu,* meaning flame. It also suggests Lusios, a divine title of Greek deities, meaning "one who washes away guilt," and was associated with Lusi in Arcadia.

Luis was also the seat of the three oracular daughters of Proteus, a Pelasgian god. This god, like the ancient Irish god Uath Mac Immomuin, had the ability to change into many horrible shapes, and his title "Horror Son of Terror" is the masculine equivalent to the Celtic Morrigan—another aspect of the triune goddess.

Uranian Symbolism

The powerful magic associated with the rowan is pure and light; it is a symbol of vision, the kind that strikes suddenly, like a flash of lightning. And a brilliant idea that is inspirational is also the visionary aspect associated with Uranus; the zigzag symbol of penetrating light or lightning, identified by the Druids and mentioned in their rituals, fits perfectly with Uranus, a planet associated with electric and magnetic energies.

Myths Associated with the Sign

In Celtic astrology the planet Uranus was not known, being too far away to be seen by the naked eye. But the ancient Greek myth of Uranus, a sky-god and consort to Gaia, the Earth goddess, does have similarities with the Celtic myth of Celi and Ceridwen. At this time of the year, Celi was in the restless elements of nature, the electromagnetic forces contained in the phenomenon of lightning.

The magical significance of the rowan tree also corresponds with the esoteric nature attributed to Uranus.

Astrological Significance

The traditional astrological rulership for this time of year is the planet Uranus, ruler of Aquarius. The planet Uranus is associated with invention and futuristic thinking, and the rowan tree character fits that description. Uranus has been called the "awakdener" in esoteric astrology, again a very apt comparison that suggests great impulse, power, and enthusiasm. In her book *Esoteric Astrology,* Alice Bailey refers to the planet Uranus as one of the most significant influences for the New Age that will transform the conscious thinking of humanity. She aligned it with the Seventh Ray, the School of Magic, and described Uranus as "a planet of violent force, whose graduates will wield the power of the cosmic etheric prana."

All esoteric astrologers refer to Uranus as the planet of occultism—that which veils what must be discovered. According to such belief, when other planetary alignments concur, Uranus will transmit the knowledge of the universe and reveal the greater mysteries of life.

Archetypal Character

Brigantia represents the archetypal rowan tree character, symbolizing the first glimmer of spiritual light coming from external forces. The significance of lighting the candles and torches in her honor at midnight—the magical hour of darkness—symbolizes the "germination" of the seed potential contained in the rowan tree sign, and indeed in all mankind. This "awakening" transforms the rowan tree month and sign with another set of individual qualities and talents. Brigantia is also a symbol of the feminine mysteries associated with spiritual wisdom. This particular aspect is one of developing and processing humanitarian vision—the mystical experience of perception of the future. But the power or deviation of such vision can also become a personal stumbling block, promoting an eccentricity of character, which again relates to the extraordinary axial inclination of the planet Uranus.

Tree Character

Rowan tree people have visionary minds and well-defined humanitarian principles. Those born under this sign experience glimpses of the future and feel the frustration of mankind struggling towards greater awareness. They remain, however, self-contained individuals, for their vision is not always

shared by others. But they are inclined to speak out with authority when persuaded by relevant issues. A cool temperament disguises some passionate beliefs, for they need to argue their case against bigotry and ignorance. They are natural leaders without many followers, taking up causes that are often unpopular or even slightly bizarre. They prefer it that way, for "vision" is a very personal matter. Notable rowan tree characters include Charles Darwin, Charles Lindbergh, Charles Dickens, and Jules Verne.

Positive Aspects

Positive aspects of the rowan tree character include a progressive outlook on life, and humanitarian principles. Such people are kind and thoughtful, but they find it hard to tolerate authority in the restrictive or repressive role; governments or any authoritative powers are usually targeted. But if they are approached on a personal level, rowan tree characters will listen politely, being the most ardent supporters of free speech and of the mutual respect of adversaries.

Negative Aspects

These are centered on the rowan tree character's unpredictable response or reaction to a situation. In trying to be completely unconventional, they may upset people close to them, and generally antagonize people or escalate a situation out of all proportion. They can also become extremely tactless in their speech and manner when expressing their controversial opinions.

General

With regard to their careers, rowan tree characters are unusually clever people, with skills and talents of a specialized and unique caliber. This particular aspect of character sets them apart from others and, although some may be employed in ordinary careers, it will become obvious sooner or later that they have changed the rule book to suit themselves. They are naturally drawn to modern technology and methods, and the overwhelming desire is to reorganize completely any system or method considered to be outdated.

Because of their original abilities they rise to and obtain high positions, despite their unconventional attitudes, but they do not court power or promotion. They make sympathetic bosses, but don't like taking responsibility for others. They often belong to elite groups or professional associations, but always retain their individual status or way of thinking.

They will have some diverse interests, from birdwatching to playing bongo drums. They are musically inclined, and usually prefer modern or fairly obscure composers. They tinker with everything, from mechanics to electrics, and are the original DIY exponents. They are extremely inventive people and enjoy utilizing what other people will discard. The "absent-minded professor" is a good analogy; it sums up the impression they create generally. In a world of illusion, however, who are they when they are not trying to appear so eccentric or cranky? A good question, but the rowan tree characters will have the answers. Ask them, and learn something quite riveting.

Their sense of humor is very odd indeed. They tend to laugh at the serious issues of life, which can be a bit disconcerting, to say the least. Perhaps because they see everything in a different perspective, the issues that appear serious to others fail to impress them. This "alien aspect" certainly makes them candidates for the theory of space aliens who have landed here by mistake. They are, needless to say, very drawn to science fiction and the idea of UFOs.

Their general appearance is worth noting; they are people who stand out in a crowd, quite literally, due to an unusual and assorted wardrobe.

Love Life

In personal relationships their unpredicrability is a weak point. Generally speaking, they are determined, if somewhat unromantic, lovers. With regard to marriage, like birch tree characters, they won't marry too quickly, but for different reasons. Basically, they enjoy a great deal of personal freedom and are reluctant to change their ways to suit another, so they will have to be very sure that their intended partner fully understands this point. Marriage can, however, be extremely successful if this way of thinking is acceptable to their partner.

They are supportive parents, but will expect their children, like them, to become independent at an early age.

Summary

There is an evolving spirit connected with the rowan tree that makes this the most incomprehensible of signs. The fact is that they hate conformity, so any descriptive analysis will fall short of the mark in their eyes. If they have to agree with anything, they will agree to differ. This may sound uncomplimentary, but they are the necessary catalysts who create a new level of thinking. It is their ingenuity that prods new progress but that alarms the traditionalists. The sheer force of their persistence is amazing to behold at times.

Life is never dull when rowan tree people appear on the scene. They represent the diverse energies of life—people you can never set a watch by or associate with any consistency. Their lifestyle is certainly different to everyone else's—they tend to live in unconventional residences in unfashionable areas. In short, they are rather unique individuals who breathe a breath of fresh air into stale or stuffy environments, and their provocative style confounds apathy.

CHAPTER THREE

THE ASH TREE

NION

February 18 – March 17

Symbolizing: *The planet Neptune*

Gemstone: *Coral*

Flower: *Wood anemone*

Archetypal Character: *Lir, sea-god*

"I am a wind on deep waters"

The Illustration

The ash is a tree of imposing grace, tall and handsome, with its black spiral buds that remain tightly coiled and resemble tiny sea serpents. The pale golden light of the Sun is also breaking through the dark rain clouds with a smile of pending victory.

But the ash is primarily a tree of sea power, depicted by the magnificent figure of Lir, a sea-god, and one of the ruling divinities in Celtic legend. Holding aloft his trident spear, he commands the waters to abate as he drives two proud seahorses onwards across a stormy sea. With his long hair and beard entwined with seaweed and his blue-green skin, he represents the mystical fusion of man and God through the medium or element of water, but he remains a creature of the sea. Two black and white gulls seek shelter from a stormy sea, as the tiny wood anemone peep out from behind the rocky crevices.

Coral

Strictly speaking, coral is not a gemstone, but a rock-like substance formed from a marine skeleton. It has been used as a magic amulet throughout history, and in many parts of the world. To the Celts, the obvious association with the sea made it a favorite talisman against drowning, but they also used it to make jewelry. In medieval Europe, coral was of great importance to the alchemists in the search for the elixir of life. To the ancient Greeks its importance in curing ailments or disease was derived from its association with Perseus; they believed that coral had been formed from the blood of the decapitated head of Medusa, which had dripped into the sea after Perseus had slain her.

Coral is one of many substances reputed to have a sympathy with the wearer. The attractive deep-pink color is said to fade and dim when the owner is ill, and to change color when faced with danger.

The Black and White Gull

The black and white gull, or common tern, sometimes called the sea swallow, is a migratory bird belonging to the family of gulls and terns. All swallows and gulls are prophetic birds regarding bad weather, and ancient mariners watched their flight closely for any change of direction, for a storm was certain to blow up from the area from where they had changed course.

Lir

Lir was a powerful deity who represented the mystical qualities of God and man, as well as the mystical union of creation. The idea of a creation myth or world myth appears to be missing in early Celtic literature, but the zoomorphic and anthropomorphic ornaments based on different forms of humans and animals (as well as birds and reptiles) attributed to Celtic art reveal a definite association with spiritual and physical union on an evolutionary level. Accordingly, they saw their own creation as a slow process, one that not only spanned many mythological ages but had also evolved from the very breath of the surrounding elements. What is confusing is that they tended to personalize and integrate both cosmic and earthly phenomena into the same myths and legends of their kings and queens.

The Wood Anemone

This is one of the earliest spring flowers, flowering around mid-March. It is also known by the enchanting name of the windflower, as the March winds appear to force the tiny flowers to open or blossom early.

The association with the wind is a significant part of the mythology relating to the month of the ash. In the poem "The Song of Amergin," a short introduction to the mythical meaning of the letter-month of the ash begins, "I am a wind on deep waters," and is the quote that heads the beginning of this chapter. It evokes the "wind" or spirit God as an element of water, the four elements being known as the four winds or four spirits of God in Druidic cosmology.

The anemone derives its name from the Greek word *anemos* meaning wind, for in Greek mythology the flower sprang from the tears of Venus as she wandered through the woodlands weeping for the death of Adonis. In Egyptian and Chinese mythology it is also a flower of death and ill-omen. The Celts and Romans, however, revered the tiny plant, and it was used as a charm against fever and disease.

Old herbalists made a compound from the juice of its roots and leaves, for headaches and rheumatic gout. As a cure for leprosy, Gerald, a noted herbalist, recommended a decoction of anemone to be used to bathe the body.

The Ash Tree

Known as the common ash or weeping ash, this tree belongs to the olive tribe, *Oleaceae,* and has an ancient mythology associated with many legends of Celtic and northern European origin.

The ash was so highly regarded in Ireland that three of the five magic trees that symbolized the triumph of Christianity over paganism were ashes, the other two being the yew and the oak. A descendant of one of them, the sacred ash of Creevna at Killura, was still standing in the nineteenth century; its wood was used as a charm against drowning and was carried by Irish emigrants to America.

The great ash, Ygdrasill, sacred to Woden in Norse mythology, was associated with sky-gods, and its roots and branches were believed to extend through the universe. The Norse word *yggr,* from which Ygdrasill is derived, originated from the Greek word *hygra,* and meant sea or wet element, for in ancient Greece the ash was sacred to Poseidon, their sea-god. In Greek mythology the ash-spirits were believed to have sprung from the blood of the sky-god Uranus when Cronos castrated him.

In Celtic myth the ash was sacred to Gwydion as a tree of enchantment, from whose twigs he made his wands. A Druidical wand, made from ash, with a spiral decoration, was part of an archaeological find in Anglesey during the latter part of this century, and dated from the early first century A.D.

During the third month of the year the Irish and Welsh Celts used the wood of the ash to make their oars and replace any damaged coracle slates. The wood is impervious to water, and is therefore very durable for all kinds of shipbuilding and furniture

making. The ash matures more rapidly than the oak and, as a timber tree, was valuable for its quick growth. It makes the toughest and most elastic timber, and can be used for more purposes than the wood of other trees. Ancient people, including the Celts, used it for making their spears and bows, so that the cruelty of the ash mentioned in the "Battle of Trees" becomes clear. But there is another deadly aspect associated with the ash, for its roots are said to strangle other trees.

The Celts used the ash mainly for its valuable wood, but there are two curative uses associated with Druidic remedies that are still used today in the country regions of Wales and Cornwall by folklore herbalists. The juice of the leaf is prescribed for snake bites, which concurs with a statement from the Roman naturalist Pliny, who remarked on the virtue of ash leaves as being so great that "serpents dare not touch the morning and evening shadows of the tree." The ash also has a reputation for curing warts; each wart must be pricked with a new pin that has been thrust into the tree, and the pins are then replaced in the tree with a charming spell, "Ashen tree, ashen tree, pray buy these warts of me."

Nion

The Irish Gaelic word for heaven is *nionon,* and relates to the Gaulish goddess On-Niona, who was worshipped in ash groves. It may be further compared to Niobe, a daughter of Tantalus in Greek mythology, whose children were slain by Apollo and his twin sister Diana after she had unwisely boasted of them to the gods. Although turned to stone, she continued to weep for them. Her sad story is an allegory: Niobe, the mother, represents winter, hard, cold, and proud; Apollo's deadly arrows, the sunbeams, slay her children, the winter months; and her tears are emblems of the natural thaw that comes in spring, when winter's pride has melted.

The month of the ash is the last month of winter in the Celtic calendar.

Neptunian Symbolism

The black and white gulls and the sea-god Lir are symbols of the dual aspect of the sign, and of the powerful alternation of day and night, which had a profound meaning for the Celts. This fundamental duality formed their two worlds of dimensions of being—the Other World of the Sidhe (pronounced shee) and the world of mortals inhabited by man.

The Other World should not be confused with the underworld (Annwn, an astral plane of initiation), as is often the case. The former was a place where time had a different dimension, but which existed as a physical reality. It was the home of their gods and the immortal spirits of their ancestors, the Sidhe or faery people. It was a place of light and laughter, love and great joy. Life was enhanced in every sense, a place where everyone could achieve their dreams.

The journey to reach the Other World usually

involved traveling across water, with a compass bearing of due west, to the farthest westward point, where the Other World Islands lay. These Islands had a strange variety of names and provided many experiences to encounter, but the outcome was mostly favorable for the traveler brave enough to journey there.

Another form of entry into the Other World was finding a doorway or portal where both worlds met. Natural earth mounds were considered the most likely entrances, and relate to the Celts' mysterious subterranean god, Dis. There are numerous stories and legends of people accidentally falling down these shafts, and these voyages of discovery had significant meaning and purpose. The experience brought about subtle changes within the human psyche and the person concerned developed their personal potential to the full—and then some. Wisdom and knowledge were always gained, but the gifts from the Other World were primarily artistic—a beautiful singing voice or the talent for writing poetry or music. Their most precious gift, however, was the gift of healing; this was a spiritual gift, and one that related very positively to the sign of the ash tree.

It was when people returned from the Other World that time and space somehow collided. What had seemed a short visit, a matter of days, became transformed into many years. Family and friends were now old, while the traveler remained young. Or the reverse occurred; a journey of several months became transformed into no time at all. The consistency of these stories and legends suggest the intriguing possibility of time travel being visualized by the ancient Celts, who had an awareness of a dimension of the human psyche that predates any comparative study of human psychology in the western world.

If the Other World had a pre-Christian vision of heaven, the underworld was certainly not a gloomy place, unlike the idea of hell. It was a place where souls waited for the chance of the rebirth that formed part of the evolutionary process of the soul in the Druidic tradition. According to this mystic tradition, the soul had its beginning in Annwn and then proceeded to the circle of Abred (mortal existence), eventually reaching the circle of Gwynvyd (perfect union with God).

Although this doctrine of belief had evolved within the Druidic structure of religion and philosophy, the realm of Annwn had a more ancient origin. When the first Celtic people (the Milesians) invaded Ireland and Britain they found a powerful religion already in place, with a priesthood who had erected the imposing stone monuments and tombs in order to observe a religion known as the Cult of the Dead. It took a powerful hold on the imagination of the Celts, who adapted the basic principles and grafted upon it their own mythology. But there followed, not surprisingly, a battle for religious and intellectual mastery, recorded in the epic poem of *Cad Goddeu* (Battle of the Trees). The armies of King Arawn of Annwn were eventually defeated, but the ancient British king was not subjugated. Two distinct deities emerged, known as the gods of the House of Don and the gods of the House of Lir, which became united when Don's daughter Penardun married the sea-god Lir. Both houses contained many integrated qualities associated with solar and lunar deities and infer, on a mortal level, an infusion of bloodlines with one more ancient than the other.

Myths Associated with the Sign

The Celts' ancient tradition of recording their history and sacred beliefs was an oral one, committed to the memory of their bards and the Druids. Prior to settling in the British Isles and parts of Europe, they had a very nomadic existence that probably prompted this tradition; the ancient Egyptians had referred to them as a roaming people, "the People of the Sea," as far back as 2000 B.C.

The Irish Druids later recorded their own origins and evolution as a series of mythological invasions. Their mythical undersea home was Lochlann, ruled over by the god Tethra, supreme deity of the Formorians. Tethra is closely related to a Pelasgian sea-goddess called Thetis, mother of the Tritons, the half-man and half-fish people of the sea. All Celts maintained a fundamental belief that they were the descendants of Dis, another underworld deity, and that all life came originally from the sea.

This association with subterranean gods and sea-gods corresponds very closely with the Egyptian concept of creation. In their world myth, the beginning of creation started with Nu, god of the watery abyss, who emerged after a global deluge. Again the shadow of Atlantis unfolds a mysterious cloak that became symbolic of Manannan, son of Lir. While Lir symbolized the primordial deep, the vast impersonal presence of the sea, his son Manannan became the most popular marine deity, akin to the great magician Gwydion, one of the gods of Don. Manannan was, however, a much more powerful deity. He was not only a master of tricks and illusions, but the owner of many magical possessions. His boat, called the Ocean-Sweeper, sailed without oar or sail, controlled only by the thought of the navigator. His steed, Aonbarr, could travel on land and sea with equal speed. The Answerer was the name of his sword, which cut through any armor and weapons. He wore a great cloak that could change to any color or element, and which made the wearer invisible. The Isle of Man was his throne or seat of power, from whence it was named. From there he protected the land of Erin (Ireland) by opposing any invaders who tried to cross the Irish Sea. His thunderous footsteps and the flapping of his mighty cloak produced the fierce winds and storms that deterred them.

Astrological Significance

The astrological association with the month of the ash is undoubtedly the planet Neptune. Traditionally, Neptune is not only associated with maritime matters, but governs both artistic and religious inspiration, the nebulous qualities of character that can be difficult to determine. Drugs and poisons are also associated with Neptune, the adverse effects of which Neptunian people tend to suffer from. This highlights their sensitivity and vulnerability.

In esoteric astrology, Neptune represents the

planet of chaos, a state of disorder, without shape or definite form, not unlike the mythical sea-god of the Celts. In the mythology associated with the planets, Neptune also had some mysterious influence in connection with the flood during the Atlantean period that produced the preceding earthquake. This does not mean that Neptune is a destructive force, or a force of chaos, but it does imply that Neptune has little or no direct influence over the physical plane; it is a sphere of influence largely confined to the psychic or emotional plane. It also relates to magic, which can be black or white, not the pure white magic of the rowan tree.

According to Alan Leo, a noted esoteric astrologer, there is more than one element contained in Neptune, those of fire and water, which represent the higher and lower emotions. Alice Bailey refers to Neptune as the "Initiator," the great teacher of the west, the present world initiator being Christ who is referred to as Neptune and whose symbol was the two fishes (Pisces). She also refers to Neptune as the "Heart of the Sun" when describing the three aspects of the Sun that will bring the latent world consciousness to birth, producing the final revelation and liberation of mankind. She then reminds us that Neptune does not really belong to our universe, despite its apparent connection with the Sun, for the connection is imaginary. This last point summarizes the essence of Neptune as an influence generally. People born under this sign are escape artists extraordinaire, impossible to pin down or to extract a definite commitment from them.

Archetypal Character

The archetypal character of the ash tree month and sign is best summarized by the sea-god Lir. He represents both the duality of the sign and the third mystical element of deity, the spiritual link with the evolving psyche. Light and darkness are polarities of nature—spirit and matter—without whose actions life could not evolve on any level. But as the Sun moves in a circular motion around the Earth, so too the great oceans ebb and flow in a much closer embrace. The mystical qualities associated with Lir and all sea-gods represent the unknown and as yet still "unformed" forces or energies that greatly influence the ash tree character.

This may sound a rather simple analogy, but it has profound meaning for all spiritual growth as it removes the anthropomorphic images established by religious dogma and relates to the creative imagination of the ash tree character. The ash tree person sees a different vision to the rowan tree character; the duality of light and darkness becomes more pronounced, and they have to establish, or perhaps reestablish, their own personal boundaries.

Tree Character

Ash tree people have a dual aspect to their character. While having an artistic nature and temperament, and appearing highly vulnerable and sensitive, they can suddenly switch tactics and appear quite pragmatic. It is difficult, therefore, to decide on their true nature or motives. Perhaps for that reason alone, people born under this sign have the guiding virtue of "compassion," for they understand the baser elements of man as well as the most spiritually profound experiences. Their compassion for their fellow man extends to the animal world, drawing them into charitable works in both fields.

Some notable ash tree characters are Albert Einstein, Caruso, George Washington, Jane Austen, and Michelangelo.

Positive Aspects

People born under this sign have great compassion, and the ability to relieve the suffering of others, in practical terms by nursing sick friends and neighbors, and by their power of prayer, which reflects a deep faith. This faith may not be orthodox or religious, but relates to their highly intuitive nature that draws its strength from more nebulous sources. They are highly adaptable people generally, and will make the most remarkable recoveries from any adverse conditions or setbacks.

Negative Aspects

The nebulous quality associated with this sign can also produce a sense of unreality or confusion, with an inability to cope with the practicalities of life. They can also become too easily influenced by others, with disastrous consequences. This can lead to further isolation if they then shut themselves off from everyone. A hypersensitive nature undermines their self-confidence and ambitions.

General

They have a creative genius for making money, and yet appear reluctant to accept or exploit such talent. Great schemes can suddenly fail through lack of resolve or mistiming. Sensitive artists and improvisers of the sources available, they require careful direction when young. The dual aspect is a complex but fluid quality of their character, which allows great latitude or scope to operate. A rather amorphous quality does exist, however, that is difficult to determine, and they retain a mystical aura.

They are naturally drawn to the fantasy world of the cinema and the theater—anything to do with the production of films and shows, where they make brilliant cameramen/women, costume designers, or stage scene artists. Acting is a medium they may finish up in, but it is only secondary to their real gifts of artistic flair and talent. They often have a beautiful singing voice, but the great sensitivity associated with this sign is not really conducive to the grueling aspect of stardom. In psychological terms they are happier and healthier working behind the scenes, but the mystique of their personality will always attract attention.

The nautical world will also attract them, but

there are two definite types of ash tree person. One is drawn—almost hypnotized—by the sea or watery landscapes. The other is secretly terrified by the confrontation of water; it represents a vast unknown expanse, or an experience they do not wish to participate in. The latter is the hypersensitive ash tree person, who has less control over the dual forces within them, and who relates to the "chaos" dimension associated with the sign. But there is a definite balance of duality found in the creative ash tree person. The more the creative energy is dispersed, the more constructive and stable the duality becomes.

The career is important in establishing this stability, but it should not involve too strict a routine or be limited by certain controls. The arts generally are a good medium for the ash tree person but, with their compassionate and caring nature, they are naturally drawn into the medical professions and community work. They are also the people who help to organize the charitable causes in life and, no matter how large or small the operation, their presence will add the humanizing touch that can otherwise be lacking in the administration. If they are of a hypersensitive nature they can use this sort of work to siphon off the surplus emotional energy that is so necessary.

They are basically a very gentle people, easily hurt and yet able to absorb the negative as well as the positive experiences of life. They make very kind and considerate friends, and generally create a very amenable atmosphere.

Love Life

In personal relationships the duality of the ash tree character can become more pronounced. Ash tree people have their own value system that sometimes doesn't quite relate to the reality of the situation. It is not a question of being impractical or unrealistic, however, more a case of misreading their motives, which to begin with can be extremely diffuse. They are great lovers, nevertheless, and caring parents.

Their contribution to life is to enhance every aspect of it—a tall order that can take its toll in human terms, but then we are dealing with people who have one foot in the land of the Sidhe, the faery people. They are the romantics and dreamers of life, but quite capable of changing the pace when it suits them.

Summary

Their lifestyle can be surprisingly conventional because they actually strive for a kind of order or routine. This is largely to counterbalance the very unreal forces or energies that appear to exert a powerful influence. They never really settle anywhere, but have a great affinity for living near water, although this can be reduced to a fishpond in the garden. Their life pattern is a wonderful tapestry in human terms, and they will inspire others with their simple but impressive ideals.

CHAPTER FOUR
THE ALDER TREE

FEARN

March 18 – April 14

Symbolizing: The planet Mars
Gemstone: Ruby
Flower: Broom
Archetypal Character: Bran or Arthur

"I am the shining tear of the Sun"

The Illustration

The alder tree presents a bold face of color and warmth at a time of the year that is still crisp with late frosts. The power of the Sun has triumphed as it reaches the vernal equinox, for the days will now begin to rule the night. The spirit of the tree is aroused in the form of Bran, a mighty giant and ancient Celtic king of Britain. Armed with a spear and sword, symbolically to push back the darkness of winter, he has slain the green dragon to establish his power over the seasons. The symbolism is one of resurrection and new life. But the youthful energy of the Sun-god Bran is sharp and blindly penetrating, as yet untempered with wisdom, and armed only with courage. Astrologically, the planet Mars is traditionally associated with the vernal equinox, whose symbol of the five-pointed star or pentagram is depicted on Bran's breastplate. A hunting falcon circles overhead searching for its prey, to symbolize the restless spirit of the sign.

The Ruby

The rarity and beauty of the ruby has connected it with legends from ancient times. It has been called the lord of gems in the east, where it was said to contain the original spark of life. Next to the diamond it is the hardest of all gems, and is cut to bring out its brilliant color rather than its shape.

The Romans considered the ruby to be the stone of their war-god Mars; to them it signified nobility, power, and vengeance. Henry V of England wore a magnificent ruby at the crucial Battle of Agincourt against the French, and gained a momentous victory. A breastplate, said to be that of an arch-Druid, was found at the opening of a barrow grave at Barnham Downs in Kent; it was made of gold and encrusted with jewels that reputedly included rubies, garnets, and turquoises.

The ruby has been worn as a protection against plague and pestilence, and its powers are said to promote courage, boldness, and virility.

The Vernal Equinox

March 21 was known as *Alban Eilir* by the Druids, and celebrated with the lighting of a sacred fire from which all other fires were then rekindled. The equinoxes were important dates in the seasonal and spiritual calendar of the Celts. They marked the precise time when the length of day and night were equal all over the Earth. In spiritual terms it was a brief interlude when the two powerful deities of the Sun and Moon were equal in every respect. But it also marked the dividing line that had now been drawn between them; from this date forward the Sun would appear to have dominion over the Moon, but only in the exoteric sense. The soli/lunar relationship was not one of contest, but one of divine union or integration, a point clearly understood by the Druids.

Bran

Bran became a god of the underworld in Celtic mythology, and belonged to the gods of the house of Lir. He may seem an odd choice for a solar prince, but there are many legends and associations with this ancient god that relate to both solar and lunar deities who were deposed or subjugated during the various invasions. The intermingling of the races naturally produced an intermingling of gods and goddesses.

Bearing this in mind, Bran was primarily a god of healing and resurrection, who later became associated with solar deities. In some ancient legends he was also associated with the invention of fire, which again suggests a previous solar connection. But Bran eventually became an exiled god, associated with the underworld regions, and his deeds closely parallel those of the ancient Greek god Aesculapius, a healing god, son of their Sun-god, Apollo.

The Hunting Falcon

This is one of the three birds associated with Bran, the other two being the owl and the crow. Each has a very interesting legend associated with it, but the falcon is the bird of omen, which, according to Cornish augury, relates to doomed souls.

There is something of a fateful aspect associated with this sign, but it is primarily one of potential success being created within a short time. This is an important factor of control and direction that appears to propel the alder tree character into achieving as much as possible in the shortest period of time available.

The Sprig of Broom

This also has an ancient and fascinating history. As a heraldic device it was adopted at a very early period as the badge of Brittany. Geoffrey of Anjou jauntingly thrust a sprig into his helmet on the way to battle so that his troops might see it and follow him. The Plantagenets derived their name from its medieval name, *Planta genista,* and it was used on the great seal of Richard I. The broom is the badge of the Scottish Forbes, worn in their bonnets as a mark of the heroism of their chieftains; in their Gaelic dialect they called it *bealadh* as a token of its beauty. Other notable Highland clans also wore a sprig of broom as badges, the chief being Sutherland, Murray, and Home.

The broom is a remarkable native plant, with a vast list of curative powers and uses. The first green tips and flowers were picked by the Druids and added to a sweet wine made from the sap of the birch. It made the wine more intoxicating, and was used to celebrate the vernal equinox. Broom bushes found on tors or growing on natural Earth mounds have also been associated with the enchantment of the faery people; the heavy scent of broom flowers has lulled people sitting close by into a soporific state. All such associations have a magic and mystique so akin to the nature and history of the Celtic people.

The Alder Tree

The alder's name is derived from Old English *ealdor,* meaning chief, and relates to the office of alderman, a senior member of local government elected by fellow councillors and still considered a great honor.

The alder tree is not only native to Britain, but has a widespread habitat stretching from Europe, western Asia and north Africa, to south of the Arctic Circle. It is a cousin of the birch and hazel, and, like them, its flowers and seeds are borne in catkins. It is usually found by the side of a slow-running stream, for the alder does not thrive on dry ground. The wood was much used in olden times, its quality of long endurance under water making it valuable for pumps, troughs, sluices, and for bridge building. In even more ancient times it was used as poles on which houses were built at the edges of lakes and in undrained boggy regions.

During the fourth lunar month of the year the Celts used the wood to make charcoal for their metalworking; this was a time to sharpen and forge new weapons, ready for hunting farther from the home and, perhaps, for the odd skirmish with neighboring tribes. The bark was also used for three valuable dyes—red, green, and brown—the most famed one being the aldine red or scarlet, a favorite color of Celts, which certainly relates well to the red planet of Mars.

The mythology of the alder is also largely related to war and strife. In the *Battle of the Trees* the alder fought in the front line as a sign of its courage and enthusiasm for a fight. In the Irish Ossianic *Song of the Forest Trees* it is described as "the very battle-witch of all woods, tree that is hottest in a fight." The alder is a symbol of fire, its virtues a proof against the corruptive power of water.

The green top branches of alder make good whistles, a musical connection that is in a sense related to the singing head of Bran, an alder god. Its buds, set in spirals, are a symbol of resurrection, the guiding principle of interpretation.

Fearn

This is a name with mythological associations. King Fearn was legendary ruler of Ireland in the Bronze Age, and one of the sons of King Partholan. The *P* was pronounced *V*, and his sacred tree was the alder. *Fearn* is also the Irish name for alder.

Martian Symbolism

The Celts regarded Mars, whom they called Merth, with great respect, but the warlike qualities were counterbalanced with a more mercurial and artistic temperament associated with Venus and Mercury. Julius Caesar once commented on this very point; in a critical account he recorded the Gaulish and British Celts as being eager for battle, but easily dashed by a reverse. He also noted that they were, at the same time, quick to seize upon and imitate any contrivance they found useful. Of their courage he spoke with great respect, attributing their scorn of death, to some degree at least, to their firm belief in the immortality of the soul.

Bran represents the positive Martian traits of a strong leader in a crisis and a defender of the weak. The mythology relating to Bran does, however, reveal all the Martian traits—from acts of great courage to acts of brutal cruelty.

Myths Associated with the Sign

Bran, according to Celtic legend, was the ancient ruler of Britain, and the brother of Manannan, the Irish sea-god. His two half-brothers, Nissyen and Evnissyen, represented the dual energies or elements of nature, and were opposites in every way. Nissyen was a gentle youth, a peacemaker and arbitrator, while his brother Evnissyen loved nothing more than turning peace into renewed strife.

Bran's sister, Branwen, who was considered the fairest damsel in the world, married Matholwych, king of Ireland, after a great feast that had united the two countries. It was during this feasting that Evnissyen conspired to cause mischief, for he disfigured the horses of Matholwych, an insult so dire that anyone else would have been put to death by Bran for the dishonor it represented. But Evnissyen was the son of Bran's mother, and therefore of sacred lineage. So the horses were replaced by finer beasts, and much gold and silver was given to Matholwych in way of atonement, but he was still not satisfied and wished to depart the scene.

Bran was forced to concede the magic cauldron that, according to a previous legend, came originally from Ireland. The cauldron is itself the subject and source of many legends, and later identified with the most famous Celtic legend of all, the quest of the holy grail. But in this particular legend of Bran and Matholwych, it was used as the means of bringing dead warriors back to life or producing a whole new army of men, the only drawback being that the warriors resurrected in this manner were difficult to control, and had the bloodlust that created more wars. But Matholwych was very pleased with such a prize and sailed back to Ireland with it, and with his new bride, Branwen.

What subsequently transpired is not clear, but apparently Branwen was treated very badly by Matholwych and degraded to the position of cook. She managed to get a message to her brother Bran, sent by a tame starling she had reared. He immediately assembled a great fleet and army, and set sail for Ireland to right his sister's misfortune. When Matholwych saw such a vast and mighty army, he sought to placate Bran with a great feast. He then devised a crafty plot of hiding armed warriors in the leather sacks that hung on the stone pillars in the great hall, supposedly containing meal for the banquet. During the feast, the warriors would then attack the unarmed guests and kill Bran. It was Evnissyen who stumbled upon the plot by wandering into the hall before the rest of the host had assembled. A master of deceit himself, his sharp eyes perceived the deadly trickery. He went to every bag on the pretext of feeling the contents, but squeezed the heads of the men inside until their brains were squashed.

The feasting began and Matholwych proudly presented his son, Gwern (or Gwion), Bran's nephew. The child was passed around to be admired, a smiling fair-haired child, who melted the anger in Bran's heart, but not in Evnissyen's, who suddenly seized the child and flung him on the blazing fire. Branwen would have leapt after him, but Bran held her back amidst the tumultuous shouting and screaming of oaths. The Irish and the British fought a bloody pitched battle until the fall of night.

It was then that the Irish heated the magic cauldron

and threw in their dead, who came out the next day stronger warriors than before, but all were dumb beings. Evnissyen at last felt great remorse for the dreadful deed he had committed, and the danger in which he had placed his people, so he hid himself among the Irish dead and was thrown into the bubbling cauldron. The following day, rising from the cauldron, he stretched himself in such a manner as to rend the cauldron into four pieces and, his heart having burst with the effort, he died.

In the end all the Irish warriors were slain, and there remained only seven British besides Bran, who was sorely wounded. Pryderi, the son of Rhiannon and Pwyll, and Manannan, son of Lir, were among the seven survivors. Bran commanded them to cut off his head and take it back to London, and bury it in the White Mount (now the Tower of London). It was placed looking towards France, with the prophecy that no foreigner could invade the land while it remained so positioned. So the seven took the head of Bran and went forth. Branwen went with them, but when she reached her homeland, she cried aloud:

> *Woe is me that I was ever born; two islands*
> *have been destroyed because of me.*

She uttered one last cry and her heart broke. They placed her in a four-sided grave on the banks of the Alaw, a place still known as Ynys Branwen.

The returning seven found that, during their absence, Caswallan, son of Beli, a Belgic Sun-god, had captured Britain by magical arts and illusion. The start of Bran's exile had begun, but his story is far from ended. While en route to London, the head of Bran began to sing and make prophecies. It became an attraction for pilgrims and renowned for its healing powers. The head was then duly buried in London, where it would have stayed to protect against further invasions had not Arthur, another solar deity, dug it up, asserting the newly acquired Christian zeal for deposing the old gods.

Astrological Significance

Mars is the ruling planet of the alder sign and, in traditional astrology, a dominant force with which to be reckoned. It is attributed with the vital faculties, both physical and mental; a directive to the important motivations in life, which, if lacking or badly aspected in astrological terminology, will indicate a lack of self-assurance and confidence.

The vernal equinox was a time when the soli/lunar relationship was emphasized, and represented the primeval male and female energies that pervaded the universe. But planets also have affinities and polarities regarding personal and universal influence. Mars represents the masculine (positive energy) aspect regarding mundane interpretation, and has a powerful affinity with Venus, who represents the feminine (passive energy) aspect. In this relationship they are connected with the passions and desires of mankind.

In esoteric astrology Mars is called the energizer, a force that can be used for good or evil. It was also called the lord of birth, of death, of generation and destruction, an indication of the sexual and spiritual power that can both liberate or destroy. In Roman mythology Mars was the founder of their city and their great empire; he was the personification of their glorious and formidable power.

Archetypal Character

Bran is the archetypal character associated with the alder sign, a sign that relates to the ancient Celtic concept of the vernal equinox acting as a division between the forces of light and darkness. The myth relating to his sister Branwen reflects both victory and loss. In symbolic terms the Sun, now represented by Bran, defeats his enemies but loses part of himself in spiritual terms. The sign of the alder was later identified with King Arthur and his wife Queen Guinevere, with a similar scenario taking place.

The alder sign interpreted in psychological terms identifies Branwen and Guinevere with the anima (feminine) principle in Jungian analysis of the development of the personality. The animus (masculine) principle projects itself in the heroic qualities of Bran and King Arthur, who exert or attempt to exert the more forceful aspects of the personality. The alder tree character is therefore a mixture of strength and vulnerability—a fabled hero with an Achilles heel.

Tree Character

Alder tree characters emerge as powerful individuals, no longer bound by hidden fears but prepared to make their way in the world. The path ahead is still full of pitfalls, however, so the Moon has armed her children with the virtue of courage. So eager are these individuals to set off and explore life that they often leave behind their friends and companions. They are nevertheless staunch allies to have should the occasion arise, but they prefer to fight their own battles and set the pace for others to follow. Their destination is always uncertain in life, and a restless spirit prevails as the Sun casts its own shadow across the Earth.

Some notable alder tree characters include David Livingstone, Mata Hari, Bismarck, Houdini, and Zola.

Positive Aspects

They have courage in facing up to the difficult and potentially dangerous situations in life. Their sense of adventure may at times be considered foolhardy, but they break down the barriers that have been imposed by lesser mortals. They show great loyalty to friends and family, even if these people should be discredited in any way. Their enthusiasm and vitality promotes them as leaders, who often rise from the ranks, for they are the natural heirs of enterprise and initiative.

Negative Aspects

These become apparent when their desire and impatience for wanting everything now begins to alienate them, for they will press on regardless and make many enemies in the process. A selfish attitude is quickly developed and a quick temper to match. Their sense of humor will also adopt the barbed edge of a satirist.

General

Alder tree people are extremely physical, full of energy and the need to be active almost twenty-four hours a day. They are the entrepreneurs of life, a glamorous title that fits their flamboyant lifestyle. And if it doesn't fit, then something is drastically wrong. Dangerous occupations are their forte, and not just in the physical sense; although a high proportion may be drawn into the military arena, or high personal-risk professions, the cut-throat business world of high finance will also attract. They make excellent surgeons and expert precision toolmakers.

With regard to friendships, their personal ego rides high. Equally, though, there is a side to their nature that is highly vulnerable—the need for recognition can make them susceptible to flattery and false friends, the latter being the most difficult to handle because the true spirit of the alder tree character is one of trust.

Alder tree characters may not be easy to live with, but they provide the vital ingredients of life that can be so lacking in other zodiac signs. Polarities attract for fundamental reasons, i.e. to provide the missing qualities or strengths of character; this is therefore most noticeable in this sign, as it marks the first union and division of the zodiac. For this reason, also, the stabilizing elements will be found in personal relationships and not in the compensation aspect of career, as is the case with birch tree people.

Each sign has a polarity that is a good indication of where the compensating qualities are to be found. For the totally solo driving force of this sign, partnerships both personal and, to some extent, in business will provide some valuable anchors. Personal diplomacy could also be cultivated more to curb the headstrong traits of character. People born under this sign make marvelous competitors in all fields of activity, but if they don't win, or they hit a losing streak, they may decide to quit and start again in a completely different career or venture. This can occur time and time again, and can be exhausting for their family or others who haven't the same stamina and willpower. Everything they do they tend to do to the limit of their whole being.

Occasionally, however, there exists a very different alder tree person, one who is gentle and accommodating—one of the rarer alder tree characters, who will direct their energy entirely for the good of others and often to their own detriment. In their own quiet way they will influence others to a very high degree. They are the unsung heroes, whose passing creates a void or vacuum in life, for what they have managed to achieve is as remarkable as the headstrong character.

Either way, from the very beginning of their lives, alder tree people create an impact. The sharpness of their minds and their physical agility breed a combatant in life, not a bystander. They are difficult people to keep abreast of; most people will follow in their wake, and will probably have a bumpy ride. There is a definite pattern or statement associated with this sign that is not difficult to understand. Psychologically, they are usually very uncomplicated people because they express their feelings and opinions openly.

Love Life

The need for personal freedom is strong in this sign, but so is the need for love. A passionate nature cannot operate in isolation so, along the way, and almost at a gallop, they make conquests that divert their attention, although only briefly. They tend to marry in haste, and remain better lovers than husbands or wives. They also make excellent fathers or mothers, perhaps because they see life as a kind of battlefield, instructing their offspring accordingly.

Summary

The sense of bravado of the alder tree people is admirable, but it does tend to thin out the supporters on the sidelines. Their sharp wit, rather than a sense of humor, may also take its toll, but it will compel the people on the receiving end to react more positively. Their lifestyle is one everyone else tries to keep up with, at least initially.

People born under this sign are the prototype models of the extrovert character, and they remain intensely passionate where their inner feelings are concerned. The very fiber of their being is difficult to regulate, but they do nothing in cold blood or with a feeling of indifference. If the rowan tree people represent the catalysts for change, then the alder tree people represent the steroids or the *stimulus factotum*, not to be missed at any cost.

CHAPTER FIVE

THE WILLOW TREE

SAILLE

April 15 – May 12

Symbolizing: The Moon
Gemstone: Moonstone
Flower: Primrose
Archetypal Character: Morgan le Fay

"I am a hawk on a cliff"

The Illustration

The willow tree at this time of year is a graceful sight, with its sweeping branches in full leaf and flower. According to Celtic myth, hidden within its branches lies a serpent whose coils protect two scarlet-colored eggs containing the infinite potentiality of the world. They also represent the Sun and Earth, and form a triple alliance with the Moon. The solar symbol is eclipsed by the Moon, but only briefly, as the luminaries embrace to form a spiritual or spiraling union of universal energies.

The trailing branches of the willow form an intricate pattern that symbolizes the complexity of the sign. The branches are held by a young maiden dressed in white, with flowers in her hair; she has been chosen Queen of the May to preside over the celebration of Beltane, a fire festival held on the first day of May.

The roots of the willow tap the sacred spring of the most mysterious and awesome aspect of the lunar goddess, the Cailleach. Her face is heavily veiled as she sits on a silver throne in the dark cavern under the tree. At her feet a huge wolfhound crouches, his collar of moonstones reflecting the red glint of his fearsome eyes. There is an atmosphere of enchantment as the solar spirit discovers his sexuality.

The Moonstone

This is an opalescent transparent gem, said to resemble a raindrop and to possess a serene, mysterious beauty. The moonstone or selenite was used in ancient times and in different parts of the world as a lucky charm. Miraculous cures have been attributed to it.

The Romans believed that the moonstone enclosed the image of Diana, their Moon goddess, who represented "the moonlight splendor of night," and had the power of bestowing wealth, victory, and wisdom on its wearer. The Druids hung moonstones on fruit trees to ensure a good crop of fruit, and believed the stone changed color according to the waxing and waning of the Moon. As a gift for lovers it is believed to arouse tender affection, and if placed in the mouth at full Moon it bestows the power of foretelling both good or ill fortune.

Beltane

Beltane or Bealtaine marked the official start of summer in the seasonal Celtic calendar. However, the fire festivals also represented the spiritual cycles that connected the Earth with the chthonic or underworld forces.

On the eve of Beltane all the fires in the community were extinguished, so that the element of fire was then completely absent from Earth. The Celts reckoned their days from sunset, not from sunrise, for, to their way of thinking, the night was the primeval source of light, and it was from this standpoint that they also perceived their own spiritual identity and consciousness. So when they gathered on their sacred Beltane hill at sunrise to ritually rekindle the need-fire, they were also regenerating their own spiritual vitality. Their bonfire consisted of

nine sacred woods, from which they relit their hearthfires and then drove their cattle through the smoke in the rite of saining, or purification with fire. Fire was seen as a divine power, and the people also jumped over the bonfire as an act of personal purification and transformation of the spirit.

On the first morning of May the Queen of the May was chosen to represent the goddess in one of the triple aspects of transformation, from virgin to mother. Thus the human sphere or dimension united with the etheric forces to promote a new season of fertility and fruition. Their Earth goddess was penetrated by the phallic maypole, with the ritual of music and dancing symbolizing the coupling act—morris dancing is a remnant of this ancient tradition. There was a need to impress a pattern upon the earth, and the various ancient mazes and labyrinths depicted in temples throughout the world symbolize this fundamental union. But it also became a search for immortality by joining forces with the divine.

During the fifth lunar month of the year, the Druids instructed people "to drink from a sacred well before sunrise, wash in the morning dew and adorn thyself with greenery. To watch the Sun come up, dance around the Maypole and abandon thyself to the season." It was a time of revelry and orgiastic rites to perpetuate the season.

The dew of the May Day morning was also collected and used in the rituals. The formation of dew results from the condensation of the water vapor that rises from the warm earth in summer, but to the Celt it represented an element of the divine; dew was regarded as a magical substance, being the dis-

tilled essence of the earth through fire, the alchemy of the spiritual nature of earth.

Special attention was also given to their sacred wells and springs at this time. They represented the female organs of the Earth, with their life-giving and healing properties. The Earth goddess was perceived by the Celts, and by many other ancient people, as the natural consort of the Sun, for both were life-giving deities. The Moon, or lunar goddess, was the primeval mother of creation in the deeper mysteries of life, and had the power either to preserve or destroy life in the esoteric sense.

The Two Scarlet Eggs

The two scarlet eggs hidden in the willow tree, according to the Druidic mysteries, are related to both cosmic birth and the birth of mankind.

The Druids believed that the universe was hatched from two serpents' eggs that contained the Sun and Earth. The egg containing the Sun had a double yolk of gold and silver, symbolizing the dual nature of the luminaries. Hens' eggs took the place of snakes', were colored scarlet in the Sun's honor, and were symbolically eaten as part of the feasting of Beltane. This act later transferred to the celebration of Easter in the Christian calendar, with the eggs becoming Easter eggs.

The *glain,* or scarlet eggs, of the sacred serpent may also be identified with the Orphic world-egg in the creation myth of the ancient Greeks. Their great goddess took the form of a snake and coupled with the world-snake Ophion. The goddess then laid the

world-egg that contained infinite potentiality, but remained impotent until split open by the Sun bursting forth.

The Serpent

In all ancient myths of creation serpents were closely aligned to man's own growth in spiritual terms, and serpent legends usually relate to the aspect of transformation associated with the fire festivals of the Celts. The sacred serpent was the goddess aspect of the Moon, Ceridwen, a passive but form-creating spirit. The object of these festivals was also to be made aware of fundamental truths, but the initiation ceremonies associated with the training of the Druids involved a very lengthy and arduous preparation.

The Primrose

This flower was highly prized by the Druids, and its abundance in woods and pastures made it easy to collect. A poem of Taliesin, titled "The Chair of Taliesin," describes the apparatus and ceremony associated with the initiation of a bard. A draught of inspiration was made from the flowering primrose and vervain, and primroses were carried by the Druidesses during these rituals as a protection from evil. Druids and Druidesses also rubbed the fragrant oil of primrose on their bodies before certain rituals, to cleanse and purify themselves.

The curative properties in the plant were used to ease muscular rheumatism, an endemic condition in the British Isles, and it was also used for certain forms of paralysis and insomnia. Old herbalists such as Gerard and Culpeper also praised the virtues of the primrose. Gerard recommended an infusion of the flowers to make a primrose tea to be drunk in the month of May for curing "the phrensie" or nervous hysteria (this may have been extremely apt for the Celtic revelers). Culpeper, a herbalist with knowledge of astrology, placed the primrose under the dominion of Venus, and wrote about the virtue of its leaves as making "as fine a salve to heal a wound as any I know."

The Willow Tree

The European willow found in central and southern Europe is known as the white willow because of its grayish bark, the American variety being known as the black willow because of its blackish bark. But both have similar properties or constituents contained in the bark, which are recommended in the *Materia Medica* (plant medicine) by practicing herbalists. The Druids certainly used the astringent bark to cure worms and dysentery but, along with the primrose, it was primarily used as an analgesic or primitive painkiller for the arthritic diseases that were prevalent in the damp climate of Britain.

The willow tree in Celtic myth was sacred to the triune goddess and associated with the "Old Veiled One," the Cailleach (old woman in Gaelic). She was the "crone" aspect of the triple lunar goddess who represented the darker force of the Moon, and who later became identified with witchcraft. The Cailleach was, however, the ancient spirit of wisdom, who sometimes manifested in the grotesque specter of the Morrigan, another fearful aspect of the goddess, in order to challenge the strength and wisdom of the Celtic leaders. Such confrontations helped them to overcome their hidden fears and weaknesses, and formed part of the higher spiritual initiation of fire.

Witchcraft or Wicca, a name derived from the willow, was an ancient cult that used the natural cycle or rhythmic energies of creation associated with the goddess, although this association later became completely misunderstood with the advent of Christianity. The early Christian church at first retained the mystical powers relating directly to the healing powers of the goddess; the miracles associated with the apostles and early saints are remarkably similar to the magical feats of the Druids and Druidesses who had earlier provided the people with great comfort and spiritual strength. But the austere theologians in the church hierarchy became embarrassed by the feminine mystique associated with such "miracles" and, although the Virgin Mary was a consoling substitute, they systematically erased and degraded the feminine aspect of godhead. Their patriarchal system adhered to a totally masculine god and creator—an unnatural imbalance of the very fundamental principles of life in every stage of evolution and beginning. Witchcraft unwittingly became the secret order of resistance to Christianity and a male dominated society, and witchcraft trials were held to suppress what was seen as pagan practices, but they were conducted with the kind of barbarism and terror that surpassed even the darkest pagan rites.

The willow tree has always been known as a tree of enchantment. At the famous temple at Delphi, Orpheus was depicted as receiving the mystic gift of eloquence by touching a willow in the sacred grove of Persephone. The Celts also associated it with poets, and, as suitors, wore a sprig of willow to protect themselves from the jealousy of the "crone" by acknowledging her undiminished power and status. The willow was also host to the sacred mistletoe, which is more commonly found growing on the willow and the poplar than the illustrious oak.

Saille

The Celtic *saille* became anglicized to "sally," which means a sudden outburst of action, expression, or emotion. It may also imply an excursion or a jaunt, as well as a jocular retort, but equally it can mean a more violent excursion by troops. Sally is also derived from *saille* in Old French, which translates as "to rush out suddenly," from the word *saillir* meaning "to dash forwards," being in turn derived from the Latin word *salire,* to leap.

These words aptly summarize the spirit of the willow tree, and reflect the undefined potentiality.

Lunar Symbolism

The Celtic equivalent of a powerful lunar sorceress is Morgan le Fay, the half-sister to King Arthur. It was her formidable powers, working against Arthur behind the scenes, that eventually destroyed the unity of the order of Knights of the Round Table. Revenge for the death of her father, who had been treacherously killed by Uther Pendragon, father to Arthur, was a primer, but in the Celtic mythology of archetypes she symbolizes the darker forces of the psyche, which require greater understanding and recognition.

Myths Associated with the Sign

The mythology of the willow is perhaps overshadowed by the dominion of the Moon. There is such a vast and ancient mythology surrounding the Moon that it would be impossible to include every known association and legend. The aspect relating to the willow of the "crone" or the Cailleach is perhaps an aspect of the lunar goddess that holds the relevant mythology. In traditional Graeco-Roman astrology the first and last lunar houses are those of Hecate, "the dark Moon, She who strikes from afar." Hecate, like the Celtic Morrigan, is the darkest aspect of the lunar goddess.

In Greek mythology she was also known as the queen of Hades, wife of Pluto, and one of the guardians of the underworld—another aspect of Persephone. Alexandre Volguine, a French astrologer who made a particular study of this lunar goddess, called her "The Triple Hecate," a mysterious Greek deity represented by three animal heads. He said that "everything we know of this blood-colored goddess may by analogy be applied to the persons born with the Moon in these Houses." Hecate, granddaughter of the Sun, was versed in all the inventions of evil; she used wolfbane to get rid of rivals and knew the secret of herbs that produced hallucinations. She was indeed a goddess of enchantment and dark rites, whose magic medallion dating from the late Roman empire depicts her flanked by serpents, and the action of the lunar houses of Hecate is comparable to the treachery of the serpent's bite.

In this lunar zodiac these analogies fortunately do not apply, but the association of Hecate and the Morrigan with the willow sign does leave a residue of uncertainty and incomprehension, indicating a need for affection that is difficult to satisfy.

Astrological Significance

The Moon in traditional astrology represents the mother figure, and is associated with the maternal nature as well as public life. It is also associated with the instinctive mind and the physical form. For a more complex astrological analysis, Alice Bailey in her book *Esoteric Astrology* describes the Moon as a veiling planet who, as one of the creative hierarchy, veils Uranus, Neptune, and Vulcan in an interlocking triangle of energies, formed through the mother principle of the Moon, to nourish and feed the life

of the inner soul. But in her reference to the Moon in *A Treatise on Cosmic Fire* she traces the origin of the feud between the forces of light and darkness to the Moon.

The Moon, like Neptune, has always been considered a great symbol of illusion, for nothing born under her influence endures; it is constantly changing and dissolving. However, the Moon does relate to the powerful inherited physical traits of character and the residue of memory.

Archetypal Character

Morgan le Fay undoubtedly represents one aspect of the archetypal character associated with the sign of the willow. The festival of Beltane, which occurs during this month, also reflects the transformation process of the young woman—the virgin aspect of the goddess—into the mother goddess. This significant factor relates to the sexuality of nature and of

mankind. In personal terms it underlines the sensual nature of the willow tree character, and the powerful influence of the Moon or matriarch figure. The overall influence, however, is in the transformation or magical aspect of the triple goddess, which provides an intuitive wisdom and a deep insight into the workings of nature.

Tree Character

Willow tree characters are difficult people to get to know in any depth or detail; people born under this sign touch upon all the mysterious aspects of nature associated with the Moon. Their psychic antennae are switched on, so that they have recall to the

remotest regions of memory. Their lives are full of odd experiences, and they are naturally drawn to the unexplained mysteries of life. They can become extremely eloquent in explaining such mysteries, for they speak from experience. They act intuitively in all situations, and their virtue of resourcefulness is their great strength. They make powerful friends, but bad enemies.

Some notable willow tree characters are Karl Marx, Leonardo da Vinci, Sigmund Freud, Charlotte Bronte, and William Shakespeare.

Positive Aspects

These are shown in a passive tenacity and shrewdness of character. Willow tree characters are wise parents and counselors, and their instinctive maternal nature has a powerful influence generally, being both protective and resourceful. Although they are great traditionalists, they are also receptive to change, being quick to take the advantage. They have excellent memories; in business dealings this relevant trait is the key to much personal achievement.

Negative Aspects

These are related to sudden mood changes that promote some unreliable traits of character, such that their power of reasoning becomes blurred and lacks credibility. There is also a reluctance to forgive and forget, which harbors bitter resentment and limits future success. If this becomes a dominant character trait, willow tree characters are capable of causing great unhappiness, particularly to their families.

General

Much of this may, however, be carefully screened or hidden in everyday life, for they are usually employed in very responsible jobs and positions; counseling professions or teaching are two that attract. Initially, however, these people find it very hard to settle into a definite career. They are inclined to move residences at frequent intervals, although when they do eventually settle down they often become the leading members of society. But like the ash tree characters there is still a sense of mystery about them that is intriguing.

They may seldom express a controversial opinion in public, but privately and in their career or profession they are inclined to hold every type of controversial view, and on most subjects. They may therefore appear as being very amenable people, although in fact they have a very sensual nature that is easily aroused and liable to change, becoming hot or cold.

There are some willow tree characters who may not fit this picture at all; they really are the great magicians in every sense. They will appear as the most sober and conventional people on the surface, but will have an incredible inner life or imagination. They could be styled the Walter Mittys of the zodiac. There will be a time, however, when this hidden potential or energy will suddenly erupt or burst forth. It may take the form of writing to public figures, or taking the platform themselves in order to address the rights and wrongs of a particular issue. But they are not such radical thinking people as the rowan tree characters, for their arguments have a very personal bias derived from close contacts or past experience. And there will be periods when personal motivation suddenly ceases, and the intuitive nature appears to need a complete break from routine and the daily rigors of life.

With regards to health and well-being, willow tree people are incredibly resilient, but inclined to worry about their health unduly. Their imagination again works overtime. Furthermore, because of their interest in the health and the well-being of others, they may have enough medical knowledge to diagnose themselves, albeit wrongly. They will also be less inclined to seek medical help, being drawn to natural remedies that have been handed down in the family, and there is a danger of their being influenced by charlatans or medical quacks.

Their interest in family history practically runs to ancestor worship, and they often make a study of genealogy to add to their family archives. This also makes them collectors of memorabilia. Mother figures, or women generally, dominate this sign and provide the most powerful influence from birth to death. A link with the past also crosses through every part of their life and influences their general attitude about life.

Love Life

With all this interest in the family, it is perhaps an interesting point to make that the people born at this time of the year usually marry young and are drawn to either younger or older partners. This is the aspect of the Moon that likes to be mothered or to be the mothering partner. Close personal relationships appear to run at a high emotional level and, once married, the family or children become paramount in the affections.

However, if the right partner is found, a close bond can be formed that strikes an affinity between the sexes. There is a depth of emotion associated with this sign that is full of desire and passion that is not always easy to express or channel positively.

Summary

This lunar energy can, however, be positively channeled into the arts, with great distinction and invention. It can also suddenly activate latent creative skills that appear to change the personality.

Willow tree people are incredibly difficult to get to know because there is a kind of veil over their personality and character that hides a great deal. Therefore their sense of humor is not easy to define, and could be either totally lacking on occasions or be extremely well directed. They have a potential wisdom that makes them wise counselors and, if this aspect of character is fully operative, they make the most valued members of society.

The Moon has always been associated with people who can influence the public with the force of their personality—good or bad—and it is a personal quality with which to be reckoned.

CHAPTER SIX

THE HAWTHORN TREE

UATH

May 13 – June 9

Symbolizing: *The planet Vulcan*
Gemstone: *Topaz*
Flower: *Wood sorrel*
Archetypal Character: *Govannan, smith-god*

"I am fair among flowers"

The Illustration

The hawthorn tree is growing from the heart of Glastonbury Tor, and the whole scene is bathed in a pale magenta light, symbolizing the spiritual dimension of the tree. This is a sign associated with a spiritual quest that demands chastity and purification after the earlier revelries of the month of May. The silver chalice of the Holy Grail is held by the radiant aspect of the goddess, who represents the spirit of the tor. A warrior prince leaves his weapons behind as he begins the ascent up the hill, and the Sun symbolically moves closer to his ultimate act of sacrifice at the summer solstice. But this is still a flowering month of sweet blossoms, with nature in her most seductive robes, as the goddess prepares to bid farewell to her consort. Her crown of seven stars represents the Pleiades, which sets in mid-May and rises again towards the end of October—an important marker for the Celts, both as a spiritual and navigational aid.

The Topaz

These stones occur in a wide variety of colors and sizes. The topaz of the ancients is now usually called the peridot, but the yellow topaz is the golden-hued gemstone referred to by jewelers as the precious topaz.

Confusion also exists regarding the origin of its name. The Sanskrit word *topaz* means "fire" or "to shine." The English word, from the Greek word *topazos,* translates as "to seek and find." Pliny used the word *topazos* in describing an island in the Red Sea that was invariably surrounded by fog and therefore difficult for sailors to find (this island is now called Zeberged or St. John's Island).

The virtues reputedly bestowed on the wearer are health, wealth, and honor, as well as long life, beauty, and intelligence. The Druids considered topaz to be a stone of strength, deriving its powers from the Sun.

Glastonbury

The legend of Joseph of Arimathea bringing the silver chalice used by Jesus at the Last Supper to Glastonbury helped to inspire the fabulous Arthurian quest for the Holy Grail. The quest of the Grail, however, can be originally traced back to the earliest roots of Celtic mysticism. The chalice, like the cauldron of Ceridwen, became the vessel of the Holy Spirit of God in direct communion with mankind. Deep within the Celtic psyche this process of spiritual evolution took shape and procreated their myths and legends. The Knights of the Round Table were a chivalrous order of knights who represented the finer elements of man as he struggled to maintain the integrity of the soul.

One of the most remarkable, but least known, Cornish legends relating to Joseph of Arimathea concerns a Celtic monastery and convent built at Place near St. Mawes, and originally dedicated to St. Mary de Valle. It is said to be one of the first Christian buildings erected in Britain, and built on an earlier Druidic holy site. Indeed, Celtic monasteries were only built on such holy sites. The orientation of these sites was determined by the position of the

stars when Christ was born, such that they always face due north; this is an ancient method of construction that predated Christianity, and is identical to the alignment of stones, associated with the constellation of the Pleiades, used at Stonehenge to determine the north position of the mid-cycle of the Moon. The ancient Celtic monastery and convent also represent the earliest form of Christian worship, coming from Palestine direct and not through Rome.

The monastery was later converted in A.D. 933 into a small cathedral by King Athelstane, a Saxon king, who installed a bishop and introduced the parish system to Cornwall. In 1259, some time after the Norman invasion, a new bishop, another Saxon called Bronsecoombe, rededicated the church to St. Anthony, an Egyptian saint born at Coma near Heroclea in A.D. 251, an association that once again provides a direct link with the Middle East. This bishop is believed to be responsible for the design of the wonderful arch over the south door of the church. This arch is a very beautiful combination of two totally different forms of architecture—Norman and Saxon. But what is unique about the arch is not its age or beauty: it is the story recorded in ancient pictographs between the dog teeth, a story that tells of the visit of Jesus and his uncle, Joseph of Arimathea, to Place. Pictographs have a very ancient origin and have been found on the doorway to the ancient Temple of Denderah in Lower Egypt. They are esoteric symbols related to the *Qabalah* and later masonic signs.

There has long been speculation regarding the unrecorded years of Jesus as a youth and young man. Some Cornish historians and esoterics believe that Jesus not only visited Cornwall, but spent some of his formative years in the Druidic college at Place. This is not an altogether bizarre claim when comparing the two religions; the Druids also believed in one invisible creator and the immortality of the soul, two fundamental beliefs that provided the foundation stone of both religions and set them apart from all other races in the old world at that particular time in history.

Joseph of Arimathea is mentioned in the Talmud as Jesus' uncle, and, according to St. Jerome's translation of the gospels, a reference made to him of *Nobilis Decurio* would indicate that he held a position in the Roman Senate and was a Minister of Mines. He was also known to be a wealthy merchant with a large fleet of ships and caravans that traveled extensively to many foreign ports and cities.

This relates to another remarkable feature of the church at Place—its bell. When examined by experts in more recent times, they discovered to their amazement that it was not of a beaten metal but a cast one made of wroth bronze. This is a metal of indefinable strength or hardness, and doesn't corrode. There is no modern metal known to compare with wroth bronze, which suggests that the people who made the bell probably knew more about metallurgy than the scientists of today. Furthermore, in Jerusalem, in the Archaeological Museum in the Jordan Quarter, there is apparently a collection of wroth bronze cast from stone molds. The items are known to date back to the Phoenicians, a mysterious race of redheaded people who lived during the middle Bronze Age, 3,000 years B.C.

The Phoenicians traded with the Cornish Celts, and the Druidic site at Place is believed to be the

very spot where the Phoenicians built a small fort and temple during their extended visits to supervise the smelting of the metals into ingots for easier transportation. We know that the Celts supplied the Phoenicians with tin, the essential metal for making bronze. But copper and zinc, as well as tin, were all mined in Cornwall—the three metals forming the combination used in wroth bronze. The bell could have been either cast by the Cornish Celts under instructions from the Phoenicians, or presented to them as a gift or payment. However, the formula for casting this metal remains a mystery to this day—a relic, perhaps, from the lost civilization who perished in the flood?

Cornish miners over the centuries have always maintained that Joseph of Arimathea was a tin man, and evidence of this claim can be found on a stone now housed in Truro Cathedral. The stone was found in a Cornish tin mine and has the word *Jesus* carved on it in Aramaic, the language of Palestine in the time of Christ. Around this time Glastonbury was an island and port from which lead from the Mendip Hills was exported to all parts of the Roman empire. But the Celts had been exporting tin long before the Roman invasion—Cornish tin has been found in the alloys used in the building of King Solomon's Temple, built in 1005 B.C.

Glastonbury was not only a thriving commercial port, but was also the center of the Druidic religion, the island being known as the Isle of Avalon. Druidism had prophesied the coming of Christianity, and the Druids knew of Jesus as Hesus, a name derived from an ancient Sun deity called Hu. The Cornish and Breton Celts further maintained that St. Ann, the grandmother of Christ, was a Celtic princess. This could explain their eager conversion to Christianity far more convincingly than the power of the early missionaries. The Celts were strongly motivated in anything they did, and the power of their Druids was a formidable influence to be suddenly swept aside. But blood lineage, especially from the matriarchal side, held special meaning for the Celts, and this significant factor alone may have been the prime motive for their rapid conversion. The few Druids who at first opposed the spread of Christianity may have come from other tribes with different loyalties and affiliations.

Wood Sorrel

St. Patrick picked the delicate wood sorrel to symbolize the Holy Trinity when he preached the gospels to the Celts. It flowered between Easter and Whitsuntide, a period that marked the descent of the Holy Spirit on to the first apostles, who were then authorized to preach in God's name.

There are a variety of sorrels, some of which have been cultivated since ancient times for their curative and culinary uses. Irish country folk still make a very popular green sauce from the leaves, which are beaten with vinegar and sugar, and served with cold meat. During the sixth lunar month of the year the tiny flowering wood sorrel was ceremoniously gathered and strewn on the floors to purify the home from pestilence and sickness. The Druids used the healing properties of the common sorrel found in meadows as a blood cleanser, and to strengthen weak stomachs. It was also used as a wound healer, checking the inflammation and swelling.

The Hawthorn Tree

The hawthorn has a mythology of being both sacred and unlucky. Like the wood sorrel, it is also associated with St. Patrick, and in County Wicklow in Ireland the sacred hawthorn growing over wells is still known as St. Patrick's thorn.

In the book of Irish Brehon laws it is associated with the word *sceith* and is connected to the Indo-Germanic root word *sceath* or *sceth* meaning "to harm," which relates also to the old Norse word *skathi*. The English derivative is *scathe*, meaning to injure or attack. The hawthorn is known by numerous names in Britain and Ireland, whitethorn and mayblossom being the most popular, while its red fruit has been called pixie pears and cuckoo's beads because of its association with the faery people.

The sacred aspect of the tree in the legend of the Glastonbury thorn that flowered on old Christmas Day (January 5) and again in May was that it was said to have been propagated originally from the crown of thorns worn by Christ—a sacred, but not exactly lucky, association. Another association with a crown relates to the small crown, from the helmet of Richard III of England, found hanging on a hawthorn bush after his death at the Battle of Bosworth. The device of a hawthorn bush was then chosen by Henry Tudor to mark this victory. The hawthorn is also the badge of the Ogilvies, a Scottish clan with a recorded history going back to William the Lion of Scotland; they have a noble history and supported Bonnie Prince Charlie in his unsuccessful campaign to win back the British throne. In heraldry the hawthorn tree is in the arms of MacMurrogh-Murphy, Thornton, and in the crest of Kynnersley.

In Welsh mythology the hawthorn appears as the malevolent giant Ysbaddaden Benkawr, the father of Olwen. Kulhwch, son of Kilydd, seeks to woo and wed Olwen, but the giant hawthorn puts every obstacle in the way of the marriage by demanding a dowry of 13 treasures, all impossible to find. The giant lived in a castle guarded by nine gatemen and nine watchdogs, revealing the strength of the taboo against marriage in the month of the hawthorn.

There is a duality aspect of May that the lunar division of the Celtic zodiac picks up with great insight. The last two weeks of the preceding month of the willow are a time of revelry and orgiastic rites. This was to perpetuate the fertility of summer, and had nothing to do with marriage. The sanctity of marriage was honored by the Celts, and the favorite time for marriage was the late summer and autumn months, when the rowan berries fell from the tree and stained the earth red, a very potent symbol of future fruition. But the month of the hawthorn, which begins on the thirteenth day of May, is a time for purification and enforced chastity, this diversion of energy being necessary in order to negate the power of the elemental energies that had been evoked in the previous two weeks. The Sun, a symbol of the life force surrounding them, was also preparing to descend once more into the earth. The people must therefore prepare themselves for the work that still lay ahead of them—laboring in the fields, and hunting while game was in good supply.

The hawthorn has an ancient folklore, but country people in some parts of Britain today still associate

hawthorn flowers with the smell of the Great Plague of London. It may be for this reason, or because of other more ancient memories, that mayblossom is still considered extremely unlucky to bring into the home, being associated with the smell of death. Its powerful constituents have, however, been used by herbalists for centuries as a cardiac tonic. The Druids also used these properties to strengthen the body in the frailty of old age. Their smiths used the wood to make the hottest woodfire known, the charcoal thus made being capable of melting pig-iron without the aid of a blast.

Uath

This translates to the English word *horror*, and relates to the ancient Irish God, Uath Mac Immomuin (Horror Son of Terror), who could change into an infinity of horrible shapes. The word also relates to Uathach (meaning specter), a daughter of Scathach, the great warrior queen and prophetess who trained the Celtic hero Cuchulain in the more deadlier skills of combat. However, Uathach also taught Cuchulain the gentler art of love, but her home was known as the Land of Shadow (Isle of Skye) and only the bravest warriors went there to perfect their skills, many dying in the attempt.

Both Uathach and Scathach (shadow) represent the supernatural agents that can transform both men and women into fully utilizing their potential.

Myths Associated with the Sign

In Greek mythology Vulcan or Hephaestus was a god of fire and the forge, a son of Jupiter and Juno. He unfortunately incurred his father's wrath and was flung off Mount Olympus, the home of the Greek gods, and fell to Earth, injuring his leg. For this reason he was later known as the Lamed One, a title also associated with the Lamed Fisher King in the Holy Grail legends, a title with a sacred context in all ancient wisdoms and associated with initiation into the greater mysteries. The Phoenicians also identified Vulcan with their smith-god Tubal Cain, a name recorded in the Bible as a descendant of Cain.

There is a close connection between iron-working and alchemy, a supernatural association that links smithcraft to the initiation into men's societies in Celtic mythology. In the youthful exploits of Cuchulain and Finn, a smith plays a decisive role as an initiator. In Welsh mythology a Druidic brotherhood known as the Pheryllt were alchemists and metallurgists skilled in the agency of fire; their headquarters in the city of Emrys was located in a secret castle on top of one of the highest mountains of Snowdon, a mystical and magical place where the higher powers lived. To go there was to experience the greatest initiation into the mysteries. The secret castle of Emrys is also associated with the spiral castle of Arianrhod (also known as Ariadne), a lunar goddess with the title Lady of the Silver Wheel, and identified with Arachne, the spider goddess in Greek mythology.

In James Vogh's book *Arachne Rising* the author investigates the concept of the 13 Druidic signs with great insight and detail. In his equation of parallels, the hawthorn month corresponds with the hidden thirteenth sign of the original Graeco-Roman zodiac. He also makes some useful observations regarding the hawthorn tree characteristic of being able to influence in face-to-face communication, whether in politics or in the performing arts, and maintains that the key to this personal influence was sympathy. He then draws attention to the constellation Auriga, which lies between Taurus and Gemini, whose chief star, Capella, has been more closely observed by the Druids than any other star in the northern sky. Auriga also represented Erechthonius, the deformed son of Vulcan, in Greek myth.

Astrological Significance

In traditional astrology Vulcan is still regarded as a hypothetical planet, but it was known and referred to by the Chaldeans and ancient Egyptian astronomer-priests. They believed that Vulcan was once an important deity of the Atlanteans; the Atlanteans possessed the complete tables of his motion, but these records were lost in the flood.

Alice Bailey has a lot to say about Vulcan in her book *Esoteric Astrology*. Vulcan is regarded as a sacred planet ruling Taurus through. the throat center or chakra. According to her, the entire secret of divine purpose and planning is hidden in the sign of Taurus, owing to its relationship with the Pleiades and Vulcan. The polarity of Vulcan with Pluto, a non-sacred planet and ruler of Scorpio, marks the geocentric rising of Pleiades by the end of October, with Vulcan marking the setting by mid-May. Both are initiating forces. The influence of Vulcan lies in reaching to the very depths of man's nature, while Pluto drags to the surface and destroys all that hinders in the lower regions.

The importance of Vulcan as a smith-god in the mythology of the Celts is a relevant factor when interpreting their culture and spiritual nature. In traditional astrology the intra-Mercurial planet Vulcan is perhaps rather overlooked and ignored by modern astrologers. In the book on Vulcan by L. R. Weston, he describes the effect of Vulcan in the horoscope as being fiery, explosive, and ethereal, a summation that fits the Celtic character and expresses their own particular brand of *elan* or fire.

Archetypal Character

The Celtic smith-god Govannan or Goban is the archetypal equivalent to Vulcan, while their Sun-god Lugh also forged weapons. These ancient connections with smithcraft and the initiation of fire is an aspect of purification that relates very well to the special signficance of the hawthorn month. The combined mythology of the hawthorn and the smith-gods of the Druids provides a clear analogy for interpretation.

The association with the mysterious Celtic goddess Arianrhod adds the latent ingredient of character. The hawthorn character is primarily a combination of multiple talents, and the mysterious element attributed to Arianrhod provides the sixth sense, which equates with the sign of the willow. There is a difference of temperament, however, the hawthorn character being less influenced by the emotions; this relates to the initiation aspect of Vulcan's knowledge and skills. His ancient lineage and mythology also provide much relevant information concerning interpretation, but is perhaps more symbolic of the darker element within the human psyche.

Tree Character

Hawthorn tree characters are most charismatic, full of innovations and new ideas. There is a need for creative activity expressed in a variety of interests and occupations. People born under this sign are multi-talented and adapt easily to any changes in their lives. They are akin to the Celtic bards and Druids of old, often excelling in the performing arts and naturally drawn to the spheres of influence. This gift for influencing others is wisely tempered with the virtue of sympathy, a very positive response and personal quality.

Some notable hawthorn tree characters are Marilyn Monroe, Lawrence Olivier, John F. Kennedy, Sir Arthur Conan Doyle, Florence Nightingale, and Queen Victoria.

Positive Aspects

They have a lively spontaneity and the ability to communicate on every level or channel. They have a great variety of personal skills and a glowing self-confidence that produces great leaders and people who inspire others. Their sympathetic nature also promotes good listeners, and they make honest and sincere friends.

Negative Aspects

But there also exists a volatile temperament, likely to explode every so often—bursts of anger directed verbally with the cutting edge of steel. If they feel threatened at any time, they will also devise plans or schemes to thwart their enemies, with astute insight into their opponents' weaknesses.

General

Their great strength is in fact knowing the weakness of their opposition, but they are not ruthless people, merely clever strategists. Their strategy, however, has the definite psychic element of playing a hunch, which may involve more personal risk. For this reason they relate very well with the alder tree characters, both being quick-thinking action people. These two signs are the direction finders for others, and have all the impetus of movement rather than consolidating influences. Hawthorn people will therefore be participants in almost any sporting activity, and keen supporters of a variety of public events.

Their sense of humor can be sharp and full of innuendo, the type often missed by less quick-witted people, and a talent that attracts them to writing and journalism. Being highly communicative on all levels, the public media is an area of life that draws them like a magnet. They adapt to every situation that life has to offer, and will redefine their personal skills to a fine art. Whatever their background or natural abilities, they will, therefore, rise to the fore sooner or later.

Love Life

With regard to personal relationships, it is a question of keeping still long enough to forge a permanent relationship. They have a low boredom threshold that tends to keep them acutely aware of all the possibilities in life. The vivacious quality that attracts people makes them glamorous friends, but at times perhaps impossible partners. They have a highly sensual nature and personal attractiveness similar to the willow tree people, but a more gregarious temperament overall. Some hawthorn tree characters are less extroverted, however, and remain difficult to pin down when it comes to making personal commitments.

They are affectionate, but strict parents, perhaps knowing only too well the tricks and maneuvers that are possible.

Summary

Their lifestyle is colorful and exciting, at least on the surface, but they are often much quieter people in private—or so they would have you believe. Life is a challenge to the hawthorn characters; they intend to sample everything on offer. Their youthful appearance has a kind of freshness that appears to last even into old age, the secret being their agile minds and willingness to experiment with what life has to offer. This Mercurial-Vulcan quality has all the alchemy and ingredients of life in a flux, ever changing, never still. When they do relax, perhaps the whole Earth is momentarily on hold.

CHAPTER SEVEN
THE OAK TREE

D U I R

June 10 – July 7

Symbolizing: The planet Jupiter
Gemstone: Diamond
Flower: Coltsfoot
Archetypal Character: Dagda

"I am a god who sets the head afire with smoke"

The Illustration

The Oak tree is a magnificent symbol of great strength and royalty. Deep within its roots lies the double head of Janus, a dual god of life and death, who represents the turning of the year from summer to winter. The dense green canopy hides within its boughs the sacred mistletoe, whose magical berries glisten like pearls, and a white-robed Druid stands ready with a golden sickle to harvest this symbol of immortality, a symbol of life not growing directly from earth.

The tree stands in a circle of fire, the flames engulfing the sacrificial oak king, who sits astride a white horse. The horse rears up, skyward bound, as the roaring flames send showers of arrows in all directions. The golden wheel of the Celts symbolizes the changing face of the Sun, which, having reached the highest point in the sky, is about to begin the descent. The summer solstice, celebrated on June 21, was known as Alban Hefin in the Druidic calendar, and marked this turning point, when the Sun appeared momentarily to stand still as it reached its most northerly point.

The Diamond

In most religions the diamond is the symbol of a supreme deity. In the early days of Christianity it was regarded as a symbol of Christ. Its very name is linked to the Greek word *adamas,* meaning invincible or unconquerable. The Greeks believed that fire and water had no effect on it, and that it represented a kind of cure-all, capable of bestowing many blessings. Equally, there are also legends of bad luck associated with the most famous diamonds, for example the Koh-i-Nor (Mountain of Light) and the Hope diamond. The Hindus believed that diamonds were formed by lightning striking rocks, and the Druids also associated it with supernatural forces. Its most popular virtues are said to invoke fidelity and enduring love; hence its use today in engagement rings.

Janus

Janus is a god of the past, present, and future, of gates and entrances, of war and peace, and the patron of all beginnings in Roman mythology. The Celts apparently "borrowed" this god during their contact with the Romans, but as the Celts have also been associated with the Trojan race who founded Rome it could be from an earlier connection. Janus represented several aspects of their own gods, for in their own mythology there was a series of gods and goddesses who represented the intermingling of mortals with the immortal spirits. The Celts were opportunists in every sense of the word, eager to absorb both cultural and religious beliefs, which then became transmuted into the very unique and somewhat elitest religion of the Druids.

References to Janus in Celtic mythology recorded by Geoffrey of Monmouth in his book on the ancient rulers of Britain mention a Celtic princess by the name of Cordelia, who buried her father, King Leir, in an underground vault under the river Sore—a structure originally built to honor Janus. This is a comparable story to that of the singing head of Bran buried at the White Mount in London as a protection against invasion. In another reference, which occurs in the prophecies of Merlin and in which he foretells of the ancient Druidic religion based on the oak cult being swept away by Christianity, Merlin alluded to Janus thus: "After this Janus shall never have priests again. His door will be shut and remain concealed in Ariadne's crannies."

Janus came to represent the hidden wisdom of their ancient gods and goddesses, the head being sacrosanct to all Celts. The sacrificial Sun-gods and earlier oak kings later became synonymous with the archetypal figures in legend, such as King Arthur Pendragon. He personified all the virtuous attributes of truth, honor, mercy, and justice. King Arthur was the bridge between the evolving spirit of man and the wondrous virtues of all solar deities previously identified with Hu Gadarn, the son of the creator Celi and the bardic-god Taliesin. Other parallels with ancient world myths similarly relate to the Egyptian god Osiris and the Greek god Apollo. Janus was the son of Apollo, completing the circle and revealing a root source of all spiritual evolution.

The White Horse

This is a symbol that has a sacred origin in a horse cult in Britain long before the Celts arrived, and is associated with the origin of the hobbyhorse mummers in the English Christmas plays.

A relic carved in bone during the British Stone Age and found in the Derbyshire Pin-Hole Cave shows a man wearing a horse-mask. Animal worship was evident during the Iron and Bronze Age, the

horse being a favorite totem or tribal god. Horses were shown on the earliest Celtic coins, and the mysterious hill figures carved into the hillsides around England are predominantly horse figures. The Saxons and Danes also venerated the horse, and the taboo on eating horse flesh still survives in Britain as a strong physical repugnance.

Coltsfoot

Coltsfoot is a wild herb that flowers during the month of the oak tree, and is aptly named to complement the mythology of the white horse. An old name for coltsfoot *is Filius ante patrem,* meaning the son before the father, because the golden star-like flowers appear before the broad sea-green leaves.

It was a herb most used by the Druids for cough remedies, and for shortness of breath or asthma, its most popular name being coughwort. It was also known as horsehoof, foalswort, fieldhove, bullsfoot, and donnhove. In France its flowers are still painted on the signs of apothecaries' shops.

The Oak Tree

The oak tree of the Celtic lunar zodiac is the tree of Zeus, Jupiter, and Hercules in Greek mythology. In Celtic legend it is associated with the Dagda, the chief of the old Irish gods.

The Norse god Thor, and all thunder-gods, are also connected with the sacred oak of the Druids, for the oak, like the ash, is said to court the lightning flash. During the seventh lunar month the Druids carved a circle, divided into four equal parts,

on the oak for protection against lightning, a practice still found today in Britain among some old foresters who continue to carve the symbol lest the tree shall fall.

The oak is bound up with the history of the British Isles. A spray of oak was long engraved on the coinage, and in heraldry it is the tree most frequently employed, its symbol being found in the heraldic arms of Aikman, Baldwin, and Trelawney, and in the crest of Accrington. The oak is also the plant badge of the Highland clans of Buchanan, Cameron, Kennedy, Sinclair, and Stewart; all have a distinguished Celtic ancestry, the Stewarts in particular having royal blood lineage. Strangely, they have all suffered from the tragic and premature deaths of their sons and heirs, with some direct lines now being extinct.

The oak is noted for its slowness of growth, but is one of the largest and oldest living trees in Europe. The strength and endurance of the oak give it an indestructible quality that made it a favorite wood for building large houses and churches and for boat construction. Oak logs have been dug from peat bogs in a good state of preservation, having been submerged for 1,000 years, and then used for building purposes.

There are many old stories and legends concerning oaks. King Charles II of England was reported to have hidden in one when being hunted by the Roundheads. There are gospel oaks in England and many other Christian countries that are still used as religious meeting places for the preaching of the psalms and gospels—a truly Druidic link.

The curative powers of the oak were well known to all ancient people. The astringent properties of the bark were used by old herbalists to combat fevers and hemorrhages. Oak bark finely powdered and inhaled had also proved very beneficial in the treatment of consumption in its early stages. The Druids made a decoction of acorns and oak bark mixed with milk as an antidote to poisonous herbs and medicines. At the time of the flowering season in the month of the oak they also made a distilled water from the flower buds to cleanse the internal body, and the water found in the hollows of the tree was used ritually to cleanse the external body in time for the midsummer festivals.

The midsummer festival of fire, celebrated on the eve of St. John's day in the Christian calendar, was originally celebrated by the Celts to mark the summer solstice after the sacrificial rituals of the oak king. In Ireland it is still known as the festival of Aine, patroness of Munster, a faery goddess. She was also a lunar goddess, who inspired mortals with passion, a kind of love-goddess. Her name, from *an,* means "bright," and the underlying purpose of her ceremony was to exorcise the land from evil spirits. Torches were carried by the young girls in a procession around the fields and among the cattle and, at certain times, Aine has reputedly been seen leading the sacred procession.

Midsummer eve celebrations were recently revived by the Old Cornwall Societies, with a chain of beacons or bonfires being lit throughout the Cornish peninsula. The Cornish legend associated with midsummer day is related to a mysterious Earth goddess known as the Lady of the Flowers. In an effort to revive their ancient tongue, the Cornish gather on the hillsides before lighting the bonfires and say a prayer in Cornish for a blessing on the bonfire. They also carry bunches of herbs and flowers that are cast on the stack, before it is lit by a local dignitary—a strange ceremony indeed, but the act of throwing the flora on the bonfire is reminiscent of the sacrificial flower of the oak, the oak-king.

Duir

The oak tree's letter word *duir* means "door," and is related to the Old Goidelic *dorus,* the Latin word *foris* and the Greek *thura,* all being derived from the Sanskrit *dwr.* In every tongue it is a word that infers that doors made of oak are the stoutest guardians against evil.

Jupiter Symbolism

Jupiter, as a deity, was the symbol of ritualistic worship, a priest and sacrificer in the Druidic religion. At the time of oak month in the ritual year of the Druids the Sun is sacrificed by his dark twin, who then assumes control of the life-source surrounding the people. The dark Sun is now moving away from Earth, and the days become shorter and darker. This was seen as another initiation in the spiritual sense, but the changing seasons marked a changing solar cycle, whereas the lunar queen always remained constant.

Myths Associated with the Sign

The horse-goddess Rhiannon in Welsh mythology has connecting links with the Gaulish goddess Epona and the Irish goddess Macha. Rhiannon also provides a suitable Celtic link with Jupiter, a god associated with Cheiron, the wise centaur, a mythical half-man with the lower body of a horse.

Rhiannon, daughter of Hevydd Hen, was married to Pwyll, ruler of Annwn (Hades) but in the continuing saga of Celtic myths she eventually marries Manannan, son of the sea-god Lir. During her first marriage Pwyll became impatient to have an heir. A child was eventually born after a long and painful delivery, only to be stolen by Gwawl, a rejected suitor of Rhiannon. The women who had attended the birth had fallen asleep and, to save their own lives, concocted a horrible plot. They killed a staghound puppy and smeared its blood over Rhiannon's face and hands as she slept. When she awoke

and asked for her child they said she had devoured it in the night, overcoming them all with her furious strength. They repeated the false story to Pwyll, who believed them but would not put Rhiannon to death as his nobles demanded. Instead he set her a terrible punishment, known as the penance of Rhiannon: she was forced to sit at the gates of the castle, tell the tale to every passing stranger and then offer to carry them on her back into the castle. This she did for several years.

Not too far away, and at the same time, a man called Teirnyon of Gwent Is Coed, who owned the most beautiful mare in the world, had also been experiencing some mysterious disappearances. The mare's foals were being stolen in the night, and Teirnyon was determined to get to the truth of the matter. When the mare next foaled, Teirnyon hid himself in the stable and stood watch. A long clawed arm reached through the window to snatch the foal, but Teirnyon immediately smote the arm with his sword, severing it to the elbow. When he rushed outside he could see no one, and could only hear the sound of a loud wailing disappearing into the darkness.

Upon his return, there in the doorway, wrapped in a mantle of satin, lay a newborn babe. Teirnyon and his wife were childless, so the baby was lovingly cared for, and the colt born the same night became the child's devoted companion. As the child grew, however, Teirnyon and his wife heard of the punishment of Rhiannon, and they saw the distinct features of their king in their foster child. With great heaviness of heart they decided to take the child to the castle and tell their story. So Pryderi, son of Pwyll, Lord of Annwn, was restored to his joyful parents, the treacherous serving women were put to death, and Rhiannon was restored to her rightful position, with much feasting and celebration.

Astrological Significance

In Greek mythology, the source of traditional astrological interpretation, Jupiter, who was the son of Cronus or Saturn (time), eventually displaces his own father, just as Saturn had dethroned his father Uranus. Jupiter then fought a long battle with the Titans to rule heaven as the supreme deity. The sacrificial element is in the deeper significance of the mythology, the procreation of light being an ongoing battle with the darker forces, or, in some cases, like Cronus, with the limiting and restrictive forces of time.

Jupiter has been called the uplifter in traditional astrology. As a planetary influence he symbolically exercises a very fortunate and beneficial influence. However, there is a dual nature to all planets that can be both positive or negative. The excessive or extravagant nature of Jupiter symbolizes the extreme self-indulgent behavior in mankind. In the esoteric astrology of Alice Bailey she explains this dualism with great clarity. When discussing the polarity signs of Gemini and Sagittarius, which are ruled by Mercury and Jupiter, she describes the signs as not focused on the physical plane but on the mortal and immortal brother, respectively. It is the role of Jupiter to develop these two qualities, and to integrate the head and the heart, or the mind with love.

Archetypal Character

All oak kings are related to Jupiter and Zeus, as previously mentioned. Jupiter is therefore the ruling planet attributed to this sign, which in Celtic astrology is associated with sacrifice. The Dagda, known as the Good God, is the Celtic archetype that best summarizes the individual qualities associated with the oak tree sign; the Dagda performed all sorts of miracles to help people, and influenced the weather in order to produce a good harvest. He was the Druidic god of the Tuatha de Danaans, who became their chief god at the Battle of Mag Tuiread, when he declared that he would perform all the deeds promised by the council of gods in attendance. He became known by the name of Samildanach or the Many-Gifted One, a title also associated with their Sun-god, Lugh.

The oak tree character is therefore endowed with the multiple talents associated with the hawthorn character, but the sacrificial element mentioned in all the myths relating to this sign does represent a very different attitude to life altogether. The associations with Janus, a symbol of the deposed gods, and the significance of the mysterious cult of the horsegoddess Rhiannon, also relate to the sacrificial aspects, and provide the spiritual balance of a soli/lunar zodiac. After the death of Pwyll, Rhiannon's marriage with Manannan, a sea-god and enchanter, would also indicate that the power of the goddess continued through a more magical and mystical veil. The myths associated with all the signs have been chosen to interweave and thus integrate solar qualities with lunar aspects.

Tree Character

Oak tree characters are enterprising individuals. People born under this sign have a breadth of vision and sense of humor that can defuse the seriousness of a difficult situation. Their greatest personal asset is a sense of optimism and the ability to speak the truth no matter what the consequences may be. This element of self-sacrifice tends to make them scapegoats or martyrs, but it can also regenerate interest and further their case. A lack of discretion is, however, their weak point. Financially they are inclined to take risks or make hastiy personal commitments. But they attract attention and inspire others with their natural powers of leadership.

Some notable oak tree characters include Stanley, Lord Kitchener, Cecil Rhodes, W. B. Yeats, and John Wesley.

Positive Aspects

They have a personal magnetism similar to the charisma of the hawthorn characters, this factor contributing a great deal of personal charm. They will also react instinctively with a great deal of personal integrity in difficult or dangerous situations. They are deeply philosophical people and generous friends.

Negative Aspects

They are prone to exaggerate, a tendency that can become extremely irresponsible and tactless on occasions. They are also inclined to be vain and glory-seeking. A restless spirit overall can often jeopardize or mar their best achievements by leading to blind optimism.

General

Oak tree characters are the type of people who personify all the very best personal qualities imaginable. They are, therefore, naturally drawn to the demanding professions and responsible positions in life. They often wield great power in whatever career they are drawn to, and this power is usually well tempered with a sense of fair play. But they can make formidable business rivals, not unlike the birch tree characters, the difference being that they enjoy the contest or the confrontations in life and are prepared to be magnanimous in both victory and defeat.

There is, however, a degree of naiveté in their overall strategy, which leaves them open to criticism. This can have deeper implications, and is linked to trusting other people's judgment, and being slack in checking the finer details of a project or plan. But, generally speaking, oak tree people appear to sail through life with great style and self-confidence. They attract powerful friendships and loyalties.

Love Life

With regard to personal relationships, and in their family or domestic life, they have some remarkable qualities that make them ideal partners and parents. The blind spot mentioned earlier, of being of a trusting nature, will make them the victims rather than the perpetrators of discord.

They set high standards of personal behavior that are sometimes difficult for others to live up to, and if they are undermined at home or in marriage a great deal of their motivation will be temporarily drained or misdirected. Bearing this in mind, they also have the necessary strength of willpower to overcome most obstacles and setbacks, providing they have the heart for the fight. They are perhaps more vulnerable than any other sign regarding the affairs of the heart.

Summary

The moral issues in life are recognized by the oak tree characters as being of great importance, and this particular trait will eventually draw them into positions in local government or community adminis- tration. They may become councilors, even priests or lay preachers. This will not occur too early in life, for they have some grand schemes and plans to complete first. They will always endeavor to utilize the benefit of their experiences of life with flair and generosity, for everything they do has a purpose in their eyes. Time for them has a different meaning, in so much as it is never a limiting factor, only the reminder of completion.

During their lifetime they will manage to achieve many objectives and set in motion many more for others to finish. Their acts of bravado and sacrifice can, however, detract from the more important and practical realities of life. But they prefer to carry on regardless—a powerful characteristic that sets them apart from all other signs.

CHAPTER EIGHT
THE HOLLY TREE

TINNE

July 8 – August 4

Symbolizing: *The planet Earth*

Gemstone: *Red carnelian*

Flower: *Meadowsweet*

Archetypal Character: *Danu*

"I am a battle-waging spear"

The Illustration

The holly tree symbolizes the evergreen aspect of the whole psyche. The tree radiates a red glow of life and is growing on top of an ancient burial mound that signifies the transformation of solar energy into the Earth mother. The Earth goddess is dressed in scarlet to symbolize fruition and the beginning of autumn. She is seated upon a black onyx throne and holds the triple symbol of the Sun, Moon, and Earth. The lunar aspect of the goddess has ascended to the brightest symbol of light and, with the solar energy now fully harnessed, the Earth mother has complete dominion.

A flaming spear has pierced the earth at the feet of the goddess, as she symbolically renews her power at the Celtic festival of Lammas. This festival was an ancient fire festival celebrated on the first day of August, and was associated with the transformation concept of the magical powers of the female. The sacred symbol of the Earth, a circle surrounding a four-equal-armed cross, forms the astrological glyph and reflects all the magical energies of the sign.

The Red Carnelian

This is a red or reddish yellow translucent variety of chalcedony, a form of quartz or rock crystal.

The magic symbolism of the color red has survived from prehistoric times. Red ochre has been found painted on human bones in Stone Age burial sites, and was used with more elaborate application in the ancient Egyptian burial rites. It was believed to ensure that life would return to the body after physical death, and thus sustain the immortal spirit.

When cut and polished, the carnelian or cornelian was a favorite stone for carving religious symbols upon, and was used for crests and seals by the Babylonians and Romans. The Druids believed it was a protection against being struck by lightning, and also used it as a protection when summoning demons or spirits from the underworld.

Lammas

Lammas or Lughnasad was the Celtic festival marking the beginning of autumn in the seasonal calendar, and the transformation of the mother aspect of the goddess. Having come to fruition at Lammas by entering the Earth, she will slowly become transformed into the Old Woman or Cailleach figure who will emerge at the festival of Samhain. The Earth goddess has many names in Celtic myth; the ancient Irish knew her as Tailtiu or Tailte, a foster-mother of their Sun-god Lugh. Games and warlike exercises resembling the old Olympic games were held in her honor at the festival of Lammas. Marriages also formed a special feature of this festival, a tradition remembered to the present day.

The British Celts also associated Lammas with marriage, and with the mythical marriage of Lug, or Lleu, to Bloddeuedd, one of the loveliest forms of Earth goddess. The story of Bloddeuedd is a sad one, however, and tells the tale of an unfaithful wife. Its significance to the holly month is in the role of opposites, which enables new growth through adversity. Lleu Llawgyffes was the son of Arianrhod, a lunar goddess who apparently rejected her role as mother and placed every obstacle in the way of her son's happiness. Her brother Gwydion, a master magician, and the shadowy figure of Math, a god of great wealth, became Lleu's protectors and benefactors. When Arianrhod decreed that her son "shall not have a wife of the race now on Earth," they conjured up from the flowers of the oak, the broom and the meadowsweet the lovely Bloddeuedd.

Unfortunately for Lleu, Bloddeuedd fell in love with Gronw, the lord of Penllyn, and plotted with her lover to kill him. Lleu, being under the protection of Gwydion and Math, was not easy to kill in the mortal sense but, as in all ancient myths relating to Sun-gods and heroes, he had one weak spot or Achilles heel. Bloddeuedd tricked Lleu into telling her of his mysterious vulnerability, and then with Gronw attempted to kill him. Wounded, and barely alive, he managed to escape, and took flight in the form of an eagle. After a long search Gwydion discovered him in an oak tree, "the sanctuary of a fair lord" in Celtic myth, and with his magic restored him to his human form. Gronw was made to suffer the fate he had intended for Lleu, and Lleu eventually became the lord of Gwynvyd.

The realm of Gwynvyd was the place in the Druidic system of evolution that all men aspired to obtain, and the bridge between the months of the oak and holly marks the entry or portal. Bloddeuedd was changed into a screech owl and flew away to haunt the night scene. Lleu will also surface again in the ritual year as Taliesin, the newborn babe of Ceridwen.

Meadowsweet

Meadowsweet, watermint and vervain were the three herbs held most sacred by the Druids, who used meadowsweet as a primitive but highly effective painkiller or analgesic. Meadowsweet's Latin name, spiraea, via Greek, is the root word of the modern aspirin. Its aromatic and astringent constituents make it a most valuable remedy for a variety of ailments where pain and fever is evident. Its medical uses were perhaps the most sacred aspect of the herb, and the knowledge of such herbs contributed to the Druids' powerful status.

Sweet-smelling herbs such as meadowsweet, mint, valerian, and violet were strewn on the floors of bridal chambers in Elizabethan days. All were sacred to Venus or Gwena, the Celtic name attributed to Venus. A popular country name for the fragrant meadowsweet in Britain is bridewort, and its creamy white flowers in bloom from June to September mark a favorite time for marriage, going back to Druid times.

The Holly Tree

This is a native of most of the central and southern parts of Europe. It grows slowly, but is the most important evergreen in the British Isles. Its association with Christmas as a decoration in the home goes back to Roman times, when they observed the custom of sending holly boughs, along with other gifts, to celebrate Saturnalia. But the origin has been traced even further back to the Druids, who decorated their huts with evergreens during the winter as an abode for the sylvan spirits. They also used the curative powers of the holly leaves in the relief of intermittent fevers and rheumatism.

The holly is the plant badge of the Scottish clans of Drummond, Innes, Maclean, Macnab, and Matheson. In heraldry, holly branches are also found in the arms of families named Irvine or Irwin, and are invariably blazoned as sheaves of holly or three holly leaves tied together.

The evergreen holly, flowering in July and bearing fruit throughout the winter months, has a wondrous lineage itself, being the subject of many ancient myths and legends. In one old legend, the holly is given the name of Christ's thorn, having sprung from the footsteps of Christ when he trod the Earth; its thorny leaves and berries like drops of blood were thought to be symbolic of the Savior's suffering. It is a story that dissociates the holly with the original pagan customs, and provides a sanctioned form of veneration.

Other popular names for holly are hulver and holme, and it is still called the holme oak in Devon, and holme chase in parts of Dartmoor. During the eighth month of the lunar calendar the barley crop was harvested—a time of thanksgiving.

Tinne

Tinne is the letter word associated with the month of the holly, and is the equivalent to dann or tan, a Celtic word for any sacred tree. It is also related to Tannua, a Gaulish thunder-god, who was associated with the dark Tanist god of the underworld and known by a variety of names such as the Green Man, Jack-in-the-Green and Robin Hood. All represent the dual concept of life following death through the creative power of ancient tree magic.

Earth Symbolism

Myths are often woven around fundamental truths. The legend of the Green Knight associated with the holly tree has to do with the eternal spirit of mankind represented by the oak kings, who are tested but spared by the holly kings, representing the Holy Spirit of God. In the Celtic mythology of the holly, this Holy Spirit is identified with the Earth Mother goddess, who is dressed in scarlet and holds the secret of life and death. She is later identified in the Arthurian legends with the archetypal role asso-

ciated with Morgan le Fay, an enchantress who once again represents the mysterious powers of the female. Morgan also represents the magic of the Sidhe, the faery people, who are never far away, their presence forming the integral link regarding the Celt's own nature and origins.

There are however, two aspects of the great mother goddess that are clearly defined in the Celtic festivals of Beltane and Lammas. Morgan le Fay is primarily a lunar goddess, whose influence is highly

evocative and seductive in the sexual sense. Her association with Beltane is in the aspect of transformation and growth above the ground, which relates to a spiritual conception. Lammas is also a time of transformation of the mother goddess, but into the aspect of mother within the Earth, or Earth mother, that relates to a spiritual culmination, and it is here that the distinction lies.

Myths Associated with the Sign

The most appropriate Celtic myth relating to the holly tree sign, and the one that best describes the magical element of the tree and the virtue of honor, is the story of the Green Knight in the Irish Romance of Gawain and the Green Knight. This is a story that later finds its way into the Arthurian fables as an annual battle between the Holly Knight and the Oak Knight. In the Arthurian version by A. R. Hope-Moncrieff, a blend of both legends provides this colorful account.

Camelot, festive with the celebrations of New Year's Day, is interrupted by the arrival of a fierce red-eyed giant armed with a huge ax. His broad bushy beard covers his chest, but he wears no armor, nor does he bear weapons apart from the razor-sharp ax. Dressed entirely in green, with only his spurs made of bright gold, he is mounted on a green horse, with green trappings hung with golden bells. All sit dumbfounded at such a sight.

The giant lays down a challenge, asking if there is anyone bold enough to strike one blow at him with the ax, on the condition that, on the following New Year's Day, they shall stand a stroke from his hand. At this, all the knights fall silent, and the giant sneeringly declares that the Knights of the Round Table are bet-ter at boasting of their brave deeds than performing them. With this the king is stung with great shame and anger and, for the honor of his own knighthood, leaps forward to accept the challenge. But he is held back by his knights, all now alarmed at the dangerous position in which he has been placed.

Gawain, Arthur's young nephew, makes his voice heard above the din and pleads for the chance of gaining his own spurs. Arthur reluctantly agrees, but the Green Knight smiles grimly and asks the name of the young man with such a bold spirit. Gawain tells him his name and swears that he will seek out the Green Knight within the twelvemonth to receive a similar blow. Young Gawain then strikes a hefty blow with the ax across the giant's neck, and the giant's head falls to the floor. The giant remains standing, though, having not flinched a muscle, then calmly picks up his head and springs back on his horse. With his head held in one of his hands, he reminds Gawain to meet him at the Green Chapel next New Year's Day.

A year passes, and at All Hallows (Samhain) the king holds a great feast and the whole court make their farewells to Gawain, thinking they may never see him again. With New Year's Day now approaching, and not wishing to appear cowardly or unwilling, Gawain rides off several days before the allotted hour to find the Green Chapel. He rides fast, riding through the night, trying not to give way to his real fears. Having ridden through a dark forest, he is suddenly aware of a castle set above him on a hill. He decides to seek shelter for the night and, spurring on his weary horse, he reaches the castle just before the drawbridge gate is let down.

The gateman takes him to the lord of the castle, a tall, sturdy knight, from whom he receives a hearty welcome. Everything of comfort is provided and, later that evening, he is escorted into a banqueting hall filled with a merry company of knights and ladies. Gawain is impressed with the richness of the setting and the warmth of the hospitality, thinking his last days will indeed be merry. He inquires of the Green Chapel, and is told that it is less than an hour's ride away. But he tells no one of his mission.

He gladly accepts his host's kind invitation to stay at the castle. However, during the first night, he is startled to see the fair lady of the castle, the wife of his host, in his bedchamber. She tries unsuccessfully for three nights to entice him into lovemaking, but he resists her with great courtesy and modesty.

At the appointed hour he rides off to seek the Green Giant, and finds him waiting in the Chapel. Placing his neck on the block provided, he flinches slightly at the intended blow. The giant roars at him to hold fast, then delivers an almighty blow that singes Gawain's neck as the ax is buried deep in the block. Gawain is both amazed and shaken at his narrow escape. The giant leans on the retrieved ax and begins to smile as he removes his hairy disguise to reveal his true identity—that of lord of the castle.

The Green Knight explains that, by refusing the amorous attentions of his lady, and by the keeping of his pledge, Gawain has restored the honor of the Round Table. He tells Gawain that his name is Sir Bernlake, and how the mighty Morgan le Fay, who also lives at the castle, had arranged matters in order to test her brother King Arthur and make him aware of her powers. Gawain is not disposed to hear more about his uncanny kinswoman, and he departs after swearing eternal friendship and allegiance with the Green Knight.

Astrological Significance

Astrologically the planet Earth is designated by this sign, its ancient association with the Celtic festival of Lammas providing an authentic rulership. The planet Earth has long been suggested as a possible ruling planet for several zodiac signs, notably Taurus and Virgo, two Earth signs. But both miss the period of the year when the earth is in its most fertile season in the northern hemisphere. Its exclusion in the traditional astrology derived from Graeco-Roman sources is highly questionable, considering its role during eclipses, and the great shifts in the Earth's axis, creating cataclysmic changes that have undeniably affected all of mankind.

The science of astrology has been largely based on geocentric observations that symbolically place the Earth at the center of the universe. But the position of the Sun can only be expressed through the position or orbital motion of the Earth, a valid point to remember. The heliocentric system that places the Sun at the center was believed to have been studied by the Atlanteans and other ancient races, but is now used by very few astrologers. The Nautical Almanac gives the heliocentric positions of all celestial bodies, and this very point confirms its value to seafaring people; both the Atlanteans and Celts have mysterious origins associated with the sea, which may have considerably influenced their general observations.

Esoteric astrology and, it seems, Celtic astrology both attempt to include the Earth in all aspects of spiritual growth. Alice Bailey mentions this very point at the beginning of her long treatise, *Esoteric Astrology:*

Astrologers have always emphasized the incoming influences and energies as they beat upon and play through our little planet, but they have omitted to take into adequate consideration the emanating qualities and forces which are the contribution of our Earth's etheric body to the larger whole.

In future interpretations, the Earth's sign in the Celtic lunar zodiac, which corresponds with the ancient constellation signs starting from approximately 15 degrees of Cancer to 12 degrees of Leo, may be worth noting. Planets occupying these degrees may appear more "earthy," and the calculation of midpoints taken from the heart of the degrees, which happen to be the cusp between Cancer and Leo, may, like the galactic center, provide the true center or hub of the natal chart. These degrees also contain the heavenly twins, Castor the mortal one and Pollux the immortal one. The dual aspect of this ancient mythology is not only a parallel story of the oak kings and holly kings, but once again reveals a common origin or source that appears to permeate all myths.

Archetypal Character

The Celtic archetypal deity of Earth mother best suited to the month of the holly is Danu, known as the mother of all Irish gods. Danu was eventually masculinized into Don or Donnus, but originally she represented the powerful matrilineal succession of kingship. Tailte or Tailtiu was also Lugh's (solar-god) foster mother, who took care of Lugh's education and instructed him in the principles of government and the refinement of polite learning. Both these aspects of mother goddess represent a benefactress, who symbolizes the positive aspects of character associated with the holly tree sign.

Tree Character

Holly tree characters have a personal integrity, a special regal quality reserved for the hierarchy of the Celtic lunar zodiac. They may be less flamboyant than the oak tree characters, but they exert a powerful influence from behind the scenes. Their word is quite literally their bond and the virtue of honor their guiding principle. Their strength of character is rarely undermined, but they are extremely sensitive to personal criticism, this being their Achilles heel. Nevertheless, they invoke great loyalty and devotion from friends and colleagues.

Some notable holly tree characters are Queen Elizabeth, the Queen Mother, Helena Blavatsky, C. G. Jung, Mary Baker Eddy, and Henry Ford.

Positive Aspects

These people have a firm set of values. They are strong-willed, affectionate and trustworthy. They have tremendous powers of physical endurance and will never expect anyone to do things they themselves can't manage. Their strength of character and quiet discretion make them excellent confidantes.

Negative Aspects

They can become dogmatic, pompous, and patronizing. A need for constant attention or affection can also make them excessively demanding parents and partners. They will interfere with things generally and cause discord. A miserly attitude will also inflict unnecessary suffering and personal hardship.

General

People born under this sign, unlike the oak characters, are less inclined to take risks of any kind until they have carefully checked the odds. They may still become involved with grandiose schemes, but they will also hold on more tightly to the purse strings. This particular aspect of character, plus a natural business acumen, attracts them into banking and insurance. They are often the founding members of societies or institutions; this relates to a highly practical down-to-earth quality of character, with the ability to solve difficult problems through simple logic. There is a spiritual contentment in their nature, however, and most holly tree people have a deep and abiding faith.

They have a strong blend of personal qualities that denotes great strength of character, not unlike the resolute birch tree character. They are, however, more approachable, being an extremely generous people, in the sense of providing what is necessary at the time, be it hospitality or supportive action. Indeed, holly tree characters, like the oak tree people, are great benefactors, but they will expect the people concerned to work as hard as themselves, again like the birch people, but unlike the oak tree people, who tend to take on other people's responsibilities.

Holly tree characters, like the willow people, are great collectors, and their homes are often filled with extraordinary artifacts. They enjoy collecting a certain amount of memorabilia, and have a keen eye for a bargain; their collection will consist of obscure items that have a unique history and value. Their feel for history or tradition is a key influence on their whole approach or attitude to life.

Love Life

With regard to personal relationships they are loving partners in every sense, if somewhat overly protective. They are not inclined to have affairs at any time during their life, and often marry childhood sweethearts. They do, however, have a number of very affectionate friendships of both sexes. Because they are very discreet people, their love life remains something of a mystery, even to close friends.

They are ideal parents, tolerant, affectionate, and very supportive.

Summary

There is a very serious side to their nature, which can make them appear to be lacking a sense of humor. They don't like sharp innuendos, or laughter at the misfortunes of others, but the traditional antics of circus clowns and old-fashioned comedies will bring tears to their eyes.

They often dwell in remote places, off the beaten track and difficult to find. Or you will find them in old or historic buildings, their lifestyle appearing to slot into the past rather than the future. But people born under this sign are fully conversant with life, and their reclusive tendencies are devised to take stock or provide a necessary pause; they require this perspective in order to maintain the enormous responsibilities often placed upon their shoulders.

CHAPTER NINE

THE HAZEL TREE

COLL

August 5 – September 1

Symbolizing: The planet Mercury

Gemstone: Amethyst

Flower: Vervain

Archetypal Character: Ogma

"I am a salmon in the pool"

The Illustration

The hazel tree is a small but highly productive tree. At this time of the year the leaves are turning slowly to gold and the nuts have already formed into clusters of three—the sacred number of the universal goddess. The tree is growing over a beautiful natural spring that flows into a crystal-clear pool. The nuts are dropping into the pool and feeding the salmon, a magical symbol of knowledge of the arts and sciences.

A handsome youth sits by the spring, dressed in green and silver, a book lying open nearby as he gazes into the pool. Wisdom is not found in books, but it can be found within the concealing aspect of secret hieroglyphs and ancient symbols. Such symbols, which include astrological glyphs, are everywhere in the universe and will at times subconsciously instruct the mind.

The stalking crane bird stands erect, an elegant interloper, whose sharp eyes have enabled it to catch a splendid salmon supper. Catching the salmon is perhaps more suited to some fishermen than others.

The Amethyst

This is a stone of beautiful color variation, from violet to deep purple. It was well known in ancient times and was reputed to be the favorite jewel of Cleopatra. The early Egyptians believed it possessed a power for good, and it was placed in the tombs of the pharaohs. There are also religious associations with the stone; it was worn on the breastplate of Aaron, high priest of the ancient Hebrews, and is still worn today by both Anglican bishops and Catholic cardinals.

The amethyst is a stone of royalty and divine blessing, and has been worn by British monarchs and Arabian sultans. The Druids, along with the ancient Greek priests, believed it protected the wearer from drunkenness, and improved the memory.

The Stalking Crane

This is a name associated in Celtic myth with Gwyddno Garanhir, the Lord of Ceredigion. In the Welsh legend of Taliesin, Elphin, the son of Gwyddno Garanhir, fishes Taliesin from a salmonweir after he had been cast into the sea by his mother Ceridwen. The infant Taliesin had already been through one initiation or birth as Gwion, who had unwittingly gained the knowledge of the cauldron intended for Ceridwen's first son Avagddu. In escaping from the goddess, Gwion had transformed himself into a grain of wheat, and the mother goddess had swallowed him up, only to give birth to him as Taliesin (meaning radiant brow). This transformation aspect in the mythology of the Celts relates to their belief in shape-changing and the initiation into the deeper mysteries of life.

Taliesin became the chief bard of the Cymry (Welsh bardic order), whose role was upholding the oral tradition of storytelling and composing new material in order to record their history, culture, and religion. The Druidic tradition was basically an oral one, but three forms of writing and communication were also employed, as well as the earlier tradition of using Greek letters. The first form of Druidic writing was developed in Ireland and is known as the

Ogham alphabet, taking its name from Ogma or Ogmius, an ancient Celtic god of learning. In Robert Graves' book *The White Goddess* he mentions a connection between Ogham and the inscriptions of a Greek alphabet from Etruria from around the fifth century B.C. Ogma apparently represents a mixture of the Greek gods Cronos, Hercules, and Apollo. He also suggests that the origin of the Greek alphabet lies with the Phoenicians, the mysterious race of people who also visited the British Isles.

Ogham consisted of a series of strokes with a dividing line, and was a very easy alphabet to master, but did not allow for any depth of literary expression. It was, however, a form of magical invocation, and used solely by the Druids of Ireland, Cornwall, and Scotland. The Druids also invented a finger-language based on Ogham and it was used as a secret sign language among initiates.

Another system of writing employed by the Druids was called Boibel-Loth or tree writing, and known in old Gaelic as the Beth-Luis-Nion alphabet. It derived its letter names from the names of their sacred trees. A whole system of tree magic was developed through this alphabet and became part of the Celtic lunar calendar that forms the foundation of Celtic astrology.

The Salmon

The origin of the poetic vision and literary style found in Irish mythology was said to be from the well of Segais, known as Conla's well, whose own origin or source was the River Boyne, named after the goddess Boann. According to one legend, the goddess decided to challenge the power of the well, and drowned in the attempt. The Boyne held a mystic aura among Irish poets, and their hero Finn Mac Cumaill obtained knowledge by eating the salmon of wisdom taken from the river, a similar initiation to that of Taliesin tasting the contents of the sacred cauldron of Ceridwen.

In world myths the eating of salmon or fish has long been associated with the receiving of knowledge or special gifts. Finn, after eating the salmon, had only to put his thumb in his mouth to have prophetic knowledge and, like Taliesin, was then capable of vanquishing all enemies with both deeds and words. Taliesin, as befits a great bard, would confound his opponents with the eloquence of words, but it was also recognized that the pitch or tone of an incantation could stun their enemies' senses and disarm them both physically and mentally.

Gaelic curses, the darker side of such knowledge, are recorded in the Highlands of Scotland with an uncanny accuracy, and a great proportion of Highland families carry a curse of some sort in their history. Cursing, as distinguished from blasphemy, is or was, it seems, a Highland custom; it was considered a fine art, requiring courage, for it had to be face to face. It also required a certain patience and ingenuity, plus a considerable command of language. In nearly all cases the cursers represented the victims of great injustices, and usually operated when they were on the point of death, having nothing more to gain or lose in this life. The cursed would then have to live out their days under a black cloud, knowing that the curse was nearly always attached to their family and descendants. Places were also associated with curses; for example, the castles of Glamis and Fyvie are said to be both haunted and cursed. The

best curses often took a very long time to be fulfilled, and some of them are apparently still in operation. The doom pronounced on the houses of Seaforth, Mar, and Mackintosh are reckoned to be among the most impressive and enduring.

The house of Mar is one of the oldest, noblest and most unlucky families in Scotland. The origin of their curse is disputed, but it is thought to be around the sixteenth century, when John, Earl of Mar, evicted the Abbot of Cambuskenneth in order to build a palace in Stirling from the proceeds of the abbey. The Abbot set down a very long curse, first stating that the palace at Stirling would never be completed, the dwelling of a descendant would be burnt and his wife sacrificed in the same flames (a favorite weapon of the Druids). The palace never progressed further than a facade, and was known for years as "Mar's Folly." This famous curse appears in its entirety in Burke's *Romance of the Aristocracy,* and all the terms have been duly fulfilled according to historic reference. The last part of the prophecy was that "the line of Mar shall be broken, but not until its honors are doubled and its doom ended." A claim on the estate, which started in 1866, lasted until 1885, when an Act of Parliament solved the problem by recognizing two earldoms of Mar, and thus duly completed the terms of the curse.

Vervain

Vervain is a name derived from the Celtic *ferfaen, fer* meaning "to drive away" and *faen* meaning "stone." Old herbalists used vervain as an aphrodisiac, and thought it was good for the sight. It was also rec-ommended for a variety of ailments, from the treatment of ulcers to relieving the condition of pleurisy and severe headaches. In one old legend it was said to be growing on the Mount of Calvary, where it was used to staunch the wounds of Christ. To combat bad luck and curses, the herb vervain was used as a charm or talisman by the Druids; it was one of their most sacred herbs, and they included it in their lustral water to purify their altars, and cast lots for its use in divination.

All herbs and sacred plants were always ceremoniously gathered by the Druids, with due regard being made to the phases of the Moon and other astronomical factors. Vervain, for example, was only gathered at the rise of the dog star, Sirius, at a time when the Sun or Moon cast not a light. In its gathering the earth was propitiated by a libation of honey, and dug up with the left hand. It was also worn by their heralds as a protection against snakes and venomous bites, and to speed them on their mission.

The Hazel Tree

During the ninth lunar month the Druids used hazel wands for all kinds of divination, but mostly to find secret wells. Water diviners in the British Isles and other countries around the world use hazel rods as the most reliable way of finding water in places where it is concealed in deep wells, a tradition that may have originated with the Druids. Scotland is said to have been called Caledonia from *cal dun,* which means the hill of the hazel. Hazel rods are still used for fishing in the Highlands, a custom that probably stems from its association with the salmon of knowledge. In Surrey the name of Haslemere tells its own story, and obviously relates to an ancient sacred lake in Celtic times. In heraldry, hazel leaves are found in the arms of Hesilrige or Hazelrigg.

The nut in Celtic legend has always been a symbol of concentrated wisdom. It represents something sweet and compact enclosed in a small hard shell; hence the relevant expression "This is the matter in a nutshell." In the folklore of both England and Scotland it was a custom to burn hazel nuts on the night of All-Hallow's Eve (Celtic Samhain). Two nuts, representing two friends, would be placed together in a clear red fire, and if they burned quietly and evenly, the future was sure to be a happy one. But if they flared up angrily or burst with a loud report, then misfortune was said to follow that friendship.

In England a forked hazel stick was used until the seventeenth century for divining not only buried treasure and hidden water, but in determining the guilt of people charged with murder and theft. In the *Book of St. Albans,* dated around 1496, a charm is given for making oneself invisible by merely carrying a hazel wand and eating a fern-seed. In the Irish legends of Finn the ancient dripping hazel was a tree of wisdom with destructive uses; it dripped poisonous milk but had no foliage, and was the abode of vultures and ravens, the birds of divination. Finn used its wood for a shield in battle, and its noxious vapors killed thousands of his enemies. Like Gaelic curses, the destructive power of knowledge could be used as a deadly weapon.

Coll

The letter *coll* was used as a bardic numeral nine, another sacred number of the universal goddess, being the multiple of three, and because the hazel tree fruits after nine years. The hazel also gave its name to a god named Mac Coll or Mac Cool (son of the hazel) who was, according to legend, one of the earliest rulers of Ireland. With his two brothers, Mac Ceacht (son of the plough) and Mac Greine (son of the Sun), together they celebrated a triple marriage and alliance with the triple goddess of Ireland—Eire, Fodhla, and Banbha.

Mercurial Symbolism

The Celts, according to Julius Caesar, had gods equivalent to the Roman deities. He had been told by his own historians that the British Celts were descendants of the Trojan race, and therefore distant kin. In trying to assess their religion, he was of the opinion that Mercury was their chief god, although all Celts claimed descent from Dis or Pluto, god of the underworld. The Romans had a number of gods, and were fairly tolerant of other religions.

Caesar made several interesting observations concerning the Celts. While he tended to dismiss them as a semi-barbarous race, he obviously admired

their daring courage during battle. He was particularly impressed by their ingenious counter-moves in combating his own impressive war machines. He also noted their sudden changes of heart if things went against them, which he put down to their superstitious religion, and blamed the Druids for holding sway over good military sense.

This Mercurial facet of their character was perhaps the most obvious one, and one that Caesar had keenly identified. Although he despised the barbarism of the Druids, with their dark sacrificial rites, he was nevertheless impressed with the Druids' knowledge of the arts and sciences. The skills associated with learning are another Mercurial attribute.

Myths Associated with the Sign

An admixture of gods is perhaps an appropriate way of describing a Mercurial god. Lugh, the Sun-god of the Celts, was said to possess a variety of skills that made him a master craftsman and bard, a sort of Mercurial Sun-god. The role of Mercury, or Mugher, was more than just a multi-talented deity, however. Their Mercurial sea-god Manannan, son of

Lir, was the messenger and guide to the underworld regions. He was also a master of tricks and illusions and owned all kinds of magical possessions. Therefore the mythology relating to Ogma, Lugh, Taliesin, and Manannan provides the relevant significance and interpretation.

Astrological Significance

Astrologically the planet Mercury is the designated ruler of this sign, its association with the hazel tree being firmly established in Celtic myth and legend. In traditional astrology Mercury is also a dual-god and identified with the mental faculties, perception of all forms, memory, speech, reason, and intelligence. Depending on the position in the natal chart,

Mercury will operate from pure reason or abstract brilliance. With regard to interpretation Mercury is strictly a neutral agent, in the sense of being influenced by the inclination of the individual, or with the prevailing forces operating, which in this instance is related to the mythology of the hazel tree and the associated archetypes.

Archetypal Character

According to the Irish, the Celtic love of poetry and rhetoric originated through the inventive nature of their ancient god Ogma or Sun Face. He was known as the god of eloquence for being skilled in speech and poetry, and had devised the first means of writing. Its very first use was sent as a warning to Lugh, their Sun-god, telling him that his wife would be carried away by the faery people unless the birch was set to guard her. Ogma therefore represents the early archetypal god associated with the month and sign of the hazel, which symbolizes all aspects of learning.

Manannan, son of Lir, is the Mercurial sea-god who carried the treasures of the sea, the secret alphabet of the peoples of the sea, in a bag made from the skin of a crane—a reference to their remote ancestry—indicating the true status of Manannan as a guardian of truth and keeper of the records. He does represent, therefore, another archetypal god attributed to the sign of the hazel, and this twin or dual aspect has significant relevance regarding interpretation. While Manannan represents the hidden aspect of knowledge or learning—intuitive wisdom— Ogma represents the eloquence of speech and the learning associated with the great bards.

Tree Character

Hazel tree characters have tremendous personal potential. They become the arbitrators in disputes or debates, wise enough not to take sides but keen observers of the truth. They have knowledge of the arts and sciences, and make fine tutors and writers. The key to wisdom is knowledge, and this is the important word to grasp in understanding hazel tree characters. They are keen historians and accumulate information on mostly classical subjects. With their sharp eyes they can record a scene in an instant, and, like the willow and holly tree people, they possess the most remarkable memories.

Some notable hazel tree characters are Lawrence of Arabia, Goethe, Tennyson, and Napoleon.

Positive Aspects

They are perceptive, clever people, endowed with good reasoning powers. This sharpness of intellect promotes excellent debaters and writers. They are also great planners and organizers, down to the smallest detail. The urge to acquire knowledge promotes scholars and experts in their fields.

Negative Aspects

They can become hypercritical, argumentative, and cynical. Their inquisitive nature can also become prying, and underhanded. There is a tendency towards paranoia and a lack of self-worth. A high nervous energy exists, which needs to be constantly directed and channeled, and reflects a tense mental and emotional state.

General

They dislike the presence of false values, but often have secret personal indulgences. The critical element of their nature makes them appear rather cool or reserved, and enables them to remain outside the emotional sphere of influence. But their own emotions are only controlled on the surface, perhaps to cover up a highly sensitive nature underneath. There is a duality associated with this sign, which tends to paint a black or white picture of characteristics. But the existence of this dual image means that they can appear, like the ash tree people, as two distinctly different types of character, depending on one's own personal bias.

Nervous tension can engulf them, and they are often very prone to sudden headaches or migraines. Their physical body is usually not as robust as their mental stamina and personal endurance, but this fails to deter them, and they are great examples of the power of the mind over matter. There is also an artistic ability that will operate with flair, but it is balanced with a need to be practical. Part of this talent is designing useful equipment by utilizing what is available; they hate waste of any kind. Their ability to blend into the background or to take charge of a situation is again linked to their dual aspect of character, but, while they make the most unlikely leaders, they are clever planners regarding logistics or strategic moves.

People born under this sign are probably the most rational people in the Celtic lunar zodiac. They see all too clearly the realities of life but, as a result, can adopt a pessimistic viewpoint. Fortunately, their agile minds can cope with any extremes or inflexibility, and they are perhaps most critical of their own shortcomings.

Love Life

They make honest partners and caring parents, but they may be inclined to indulge their children and partners at great expense, which can be detrimental to their own financial security—a compensating trait, balancing their guilt or unease at not always being able to express their own feelings or affections openly.

Although hazel tree characters are not overtly demonstrative people, they are deeply sincere and this special quality attracts great loyalty from others.

Summary

Their lifestyle is usually hectic, but not in an obvious way. They spend a great deal of time doing their own thing, but it can be just a ploy, and their private life is often much more humdrum. The need to be continuously occupied stems from their high nervous energy, and an intense curiosity with life. By adopting a low profile they can live in a neighbor-

hood for years, and never really know anyone. But they appear to have a stream of people who constantly visit them, and their personal contacts or acquaintances are numerous and varied.

They have a nomadic soul that takes them on many journeys, and they never tire of seeking new knowledge. They nearly always live near railway stations or airports, the means of instant travel, but may never travel anywhere themselves. However, most hazel tree characters do tend to move residences at frequent intervals, and they will establish their own particular lifestyle wherever they live. With regard to careers, they appear to make a reasonable, if somewhat precarious, living by relying on their wits or ingenuity rather than by being employed in the more permanent professions.

They are incredibly interesting people to know and converse with, and, by constantly challenging the theories and opinions of others, their own contribution, if used positively, will certainly re-define the issues.

CHAPTER TEN

THE VINE

MUIN

September 2 – September 29

Symbolizing: The planet Venus

Gemstone: Emerald

Flower: Valerian

Archetypal Character: Branwen or Guinevere

"I am a hill of poetry"

The Illustration

The vine is not, strictly speaking, a tree but a climbing shrub, and is depicted growing over a doorway leading to a round tower—part of the mysterious castle of Arianrhod. Deep within the castle is the seat of Annwn, center of the Celtic mysteries of the astral plane. Four white swans wearing golden crowns are swimming in the moat that surrounds the castle, a symbol of the radiant aspect of the psyche approaching another revelation and initiation. The fruit of the vine holds this spiritual potential, and is associated with the Celtic festival of the autumnal equinox on September 22, known as Alban Elfed by the Druids. This is a powerfully evocative scene, with the wild flowering valerian growing as profusely as the vine, and no mortal presence to disturb the realm of Arianrhod, lady of the silver wheel. The solar spirit, transformed into the four swans, relates to an ancient Celtic myth of the four children of Lir, a Danaan divinity.

The Emerald

The emerald is one of the most beguiling of all gems. Its association with royalty goes back far into antiquity. Emeralds and pearls were worn by Queen Cleopatra, a combination of jewels she is said to have liked best. One of the most fabulous emerald crowns ever made was worn by Atahualpa, the last Inca king of Peru. The King Alfred Cup, decorated with semiprecious stones and emeralds, is now in a museum in Oxford; it was used by the Saxon king in A.D. 858, but around the sides in Gaelic letters of gold are the words "Alfred ordered me to be made." The Celts were fine jewelers and goldsmiths, particularly the Irish Celts, who may have sent it over to Alfred as a gesture of friendship. The Irish Druids considered emeralds to be a powerful antidote to all types of poison, a significant or relevant association with a drinking cup. Wearing the emerald has a similar association as wearing the diamond, as it is said to enhance love and understanding.

The Four White Swans

These represent the children of Lir, the sea-god who was also the father of the Irish sea-god Manannan. In this saga, which forms part of the Milesian cycle, he married two sisters in succession—Eve and Aoife, the foster daughters of Boy Dearg, king of the South of Ireland. Lir had recently lost his wife and there was a rift between himself and the newly elected king of the South, whom Lir had refused to recognize. Boy Dearg decided to heal the rift by offering Lir the choice of three sisters, Eve, Aoife and Alva, in marriage. All three were of identical and unsurpassed beauty, but Lir had chosen Eve because she was the eldest and possessed the greatest wisdom of the three.

Within a year Eve bore twin children, a girl and boy, called Fionnuala and Aedh. Another year passed and she bore twins again, two boys called Fiachra and Conn, but this time it was a difficult birth and Eve died. Lir had loved Eve more ardently than his first wife, and his grief became as wild and tormented as the raging seas that pounded the northern shores. But as the children grew, their own radiant beauty, the like of which had never been seen among the Tuatha De Danaans, helped to ease the grief of their father and his people. Everyone marveled at their remarkable singing voices, their graceful bodies and their gentle, loving natures, and slowly the heart of Lir mended.

After a decent interval of mourning, the king of the South sent messengers to Lir suggesting another marriage, and who could be better suited as a foster mother for the children than Aoife, who had deeply lamented her sister's sad passing. In the beginning, Aoife clearly loved the children and they made a happy family, with Lir sitting among them recounting the stories of the old gods and ancient heroes. But the intense love that Lir showed for his children eventually made Aoife insanely jealous, and her heart and mind became poisoned with a twisted fury.

This change of heart, although carefully concealed, had been observed by the eldest child Fionnuala, who grew wary of her aunt and frightened for the safety of her younger brothers. Aoife quickly made her plans, realizing that Fionnuala could be a dangerous adversary. One morning, she roused the children in the early hours by telling them that she was taking them to visit Boy Dearg. They were all excited, except Fionnuala, who tried to find her father to warn him of their danger. But when Aoife leapt into a chariot with her brothers, Fionnuala decided she must go along to protect them.

After only a short distance Fionnuala's suspicions were confirmed as Aoife ordered her servants to kill them. The servants refused, but they were frightened of their queen, who possessed the power of enchantment, one of the awesome powers of the Danaans. Aoife then cunningly resorted to a show of false

remorse to calm their fears, and they continued on the long journey. When they reached the shores of Lake Derryvarach, a lonely stretch of land in the middle of Ireland, she ordered the charioteer to stop once again, and told the children to wash and refresh themselves in the water. But as they waded into the water, she cast a spell with a wave of her wand, transforming them into four white swans and pronounced the following doom: "They are to spend three hundred years on the Lake of Derryvarach, three hundred on the Straits of Moyle [between Ireland and Scotland], three hundred on the Atlantic by Erris and Inishglory, and when the woman of the South is mated with the man of the North, the enchantment will end."

Aoife had been unable to render them mute, because of the powers of Fionnuala, although in some versions of the legend it was said to be due to Aoife's sudden remorse and sorrow in destroying the finest potential of her own race. She also redeemed the Danaan gift of music by setting a time limit on their fate. The children of Lir then had the power to rise from the mists once again and restore the Danaan traditions. But either way, it was a dreadful fate that imprisoned the shining radiance of the Tuatha De Danaan.

When Lir and Boy Deargh discovered Aoife's wickedness, the king of the South transformed her into "a demon of the air," a cold and whistling east wind, where she is said to reside to this day. But what of the fate of the four white swans? They preserved the Danaan gift of making sad sweet music, which reverberated across the Lake and reached the stars. The power of music in healing was clearly understood by the Celts, and the magical effect of

this music eased the pain of Lir and Boy Deargh every time they visited their children. It also helped to ease the pain and inflictions of their people who, for many centuries, continued to pay homage to the children of Lir.

The coming of Christianity coincided with the prophecy being fulfilled, when a princess of Munster became betrothed to Lairgmen, the chief of Connacht. Nine hundred years had passed as the four white swans landed near the cell of a saintly hermit; indeed some legends say it was the sound of the bell being rung by the Christian monk that finally broke the spell of Aoife. But after they had changed only briefly into their former radiant bodies they linked arms and died, as the holy man blessed them and accepted them into the Christian church.

Singing swans in Ireland still exist and, just as the legend of King Arthur evokes a sense of Celtic chivalry, so the haunting cry of the swan's lament at the death of his lifelong partner recalls the last days of Lir's children.

Valerian

Valerian is a wild herb that is still flowering in the month of the autumnal equinox, and the Druids used it extensively. They referred to it as an "all heal," a name that best describes its amazing virtues.

There are numerous species of valerian, widely distributed in the temperate parts of the world. Ancient people from India to Ethiopia and from Egypt to Turkey used its aromatic essences in their baths. The Druids gathered the wild growing true valerian, which had no scent, and used it mainly as a purgative and for hysterical complaints. Valerian is still used as a mild sedative by modern herbalists.

The Vine

The name of the vine is derived from *viere,* which means "to twist" and relates to its spiraling growth. Although not native to Britain, it was an important motif during the British Bronze Age. In British heraldry, the vine appears in the arms of Ruspoli, and the family of Archer-Houblon. Both have obscure origins similar to the Danaan people, who had brought the vine with them when they invaded Ireland. Initially it was successfully grown in a few sheltered southern regions, but since it could not be established as a wild plant, the hardier bramble was apparently used as a substitute; the color of the berries and the shape of leaves of the two plants do correspond, and blackberry wine is a heady drink when compared with the intoxicating grape wines.

In all Celtic countries there still appears to be a taboo in eating the fruit of the bramble, a taboo that was originally associated with the vine. In Brittany and Cornwall the reason given is that "it belongs to the faeries." In the West Country folklore of Britain, eating blackberries was refrained from after the last day of September, when the devil was said to enter the fruit. Similar taboos exist in Wales and Ireland, although the medicinal properties of the roots were utilized by the Irish Druids to stop diarrhea. During the tenth lunar month the healing properties of the bramble were considered most active, and children were passed through a hoop of the blackberry bush to cure hernias or ruptures.

Muin

This is the Ogham letter name for the bramble. The myths relating to the vine, albeit the bramble in Britain, have some very ancient origins, going back to the early passages in the Bible. The vine was frequently mentioned at the time of Noah, and has also been associated with a symbol relating to Jesus.

Myths Associated with the Sign

The musical skills of the Danaans and their knowledge of using music to heal relates to the myth of Orpheus, a music-god, who discovers his own fate when he meets Bacchus or Dionysus, the Greek vine-god. Orpheus, son of Apollo and the fair Calliope, one of the muses, had inherited all the musical and poetical gifts of his parents. He fell in love with the enchanting Eurydice, but shortly after their marriage she was bitten by a venomous serpent and her spirit conducted down into the gloomy realm of Pluto. Orpheus' subsequent heartrending laments made life unbearable for both mortals and immortals alike, so finally Jupiter gave him permission to seek Eurydice, but warned him to abide by any judgments set down by Pluto.

So it was that the magic sounds of Orpheus' lute penetrated into Tartarus, the remote depths of Hades, where even the condemned shades ceased their groaning and momentarily stopped from their toil. Cerberus, the monstrous dog who guarded the gates of Hades, sat down and allowed Orpheus to pass. No living being had ever before penetrated these regions, and even Pluto sat in silence with his wife Persephone, both moved to tears by the exquisitely haunting melody. They graciously consented to restore Eurydice, but Pluto imposed two strict conditions. Orpheus must not turn back to look into Hades at his wife or attempt to speak to her on the return journey.

Orpheus happily agreed to these terms, but his joy inevitably turned to curiosity, and having nearly reached the entrance he glanced back to see if Eurydice was still as lovely as he remembered. The form of his beloved wife vanished before his eyes, and filled with great despair he wandered off into a forest to seek solitude. Here he fatefully stumbled upon the revelries of Dionysus, and, because he refused to play for them, the Furies tore him to pieces and cast his remains into the Hebrus River. With his head still murmuring the name of Eurydice, it drifted off downstream towards Hades as his spirit rushed to join her—a bittersweet ending.

The tale of Orpheus and Eurydice was seen by the ancient Greeks as the personification of the wild music of the winds, and of the morning, with its short-lived beauty. Orpheus was also seen as the Sun plunging into the abyss of darkness in the hope of overtaking the vanishing dawn—Eurydice. Together they represent light slain by the serpents of darkness at twilight.

The autumnal equinox (Alban Elfed) was seen by the Celts as representing the twilight of their solar-god, and the sign of the vine is therefore associated with great joy and sadness. The Sun and Moon renew their relationship at the festival of Alban Elfed, only to bid farewell as the light of the Sun begins the final descent in its yearly cycle.

Venusian Symbolism

The relationship between Arthur and Guinevere also represents a spiritual polarity that requires growth. Theirs is an untenable situation, which explains why Arthur cannot hold his wife's affections; just as she is stolen by Melwas, king of the Summer Land (Somerset) in the twelfth-century *Vita Gildae, so* she is also carried off by her lover Lancelot in the Arthurian tale. Before that, she escapes from the clutches of Mordred by shutting herself up in a fortress to escape his unwelcome attentions.

Guinevere represents all the facets of womanhood, from the innocent maiden to the unfaithful wife, depending on the theme of the myth. When she faces Arthur across the dividing line of the equinoxes, he can only catch a glimpse of her and, like Orpheus, can only briefly sample a union with his bride, who is then snatched away just as he is about to have her restored to his side. So Arthur and Guinevere symbolize the irreconcilable forces of summer and winter, light and darkness.

Astrological Significance

The planet Venus is also associated with the autumnal equinox in traditional astrology. Her polarity is seen as a partnership with Mars, who rules the vernal equinox. Venus was known by the name of Gwena to the Druid astronomers, and later associated with Branwen, sister of Bran, and Queen Guinevere, wife of King Arthur. With Arthur representing the vernal equinox, their fleeting partnership symbolized the division of the seasonal year. The transforming energies of the seasons was seen in basic terms of male and female principles; the equinoxes and solstices were associated with and activated by male gods, while the fire festivals were distinctly female in nature, and symbolized the ritual year.

Venus has been referred to as the unifier by Alan Leo, and is said to represent the human soul, while Mars represents the animal soul of mankind. But there is also a complex esoteric mythology associated with the planet Venus, which stresses the duality of her nature and has been called the Venus–Lucifer effect. This description perhaps conveys this particular duality: "Venus is a symbol of external splendor and internal corruption."

In mundane astrology, however, Venus is regarded as a benefic planet, which means a most fortunate influence. Venus is regarded in these positive terms as representing a symbol of harmony and refinement, an appreciation of beauty and the arts, a gentle nature, and generally a refining energy or influence. The negative qualities are the extreme of all these traits—not the opposite—for Venus defines a receptive passive principle that projects inwardly.

Archetypal Character

Guinevere and Branwen are the Celtic archetypal characters associated with the sign of the vine, and the myth of Lir's children represents the shining but elusive potential. The myth of Orpheus expresses the anguish or sorrowful aspect of the sign; this is related to the seasonal aspect of the month, which is one of inevitable change bringing uncertainty or apprehension, and is another relevant point of character interpretation.

The character of Guinevere is complex but not difficult to interpret in human terms. The vine itself has a surrogate symbol of the bramble, yet another significant factor, which relates to the role of surrogate motherhood (Aoife) or fostering other people's children and ambitions.

Tree Character

Vine characters are an odd mixture of joy and wrath. One moment they are full of enthusiasm and exhilaration, the next moment full of suppressed anger or sadness. People born under this sign have emotions that always run at a high level, yet they can appear remarkably cool in the face of opposition. It is a great mistake to underestimate vine characters; they are the instinctive organizers of life, always ahead of the field when it comes to contingency plans. But the harmonious balance required is mercy, the ability to forgive with true compassion, for they find it hard to come to terms with certain aspects of their lives.

Some notable vine characters include Tolstoy, Queen Elizabeth I of England, Lord Nelson, and Greta Garbo.

Positive Aspects

There is much to be admired if the positive aspects are dominant. Vine people can be kind and gentle, adept in love and the social arts. Their creative talents show great flair and style. They also help to create harmony and stability.

Negative Aspects

These character aspects are excessive self-indulgence and laziness. Such people will tend to overindulge in all things, and become careless or sloppy in their dress and manner. There is also lack of consideration for other people's feelings, and they can become totally dependent on others, almost parasitical.

General

They are drawn into public service careers, having a keen sense of duty and patriotism. But their professional and personal circumstances can change overnight, and they may suddenly find themselves in an altogether different environment or situation. These apparent swings of fortune are perhaps responsible for their instinctive need of always making those contingency plans, a similar trait associated with the polarity sign of the alder tree—a sign marking significant changes. A restless quality exists within the psyche, which requires a great deal of emotional and material security to feel content.

Underneath their cool reserve and efficiency lies an extremely sensual nature, and how they manage to control their passionate nature is perhaps the key to their strength or weakness of character. They certainly have a sense of survival or a personal indemnity factor, and they will be employed when everyone else has been given notice to quit. This enduring quality or trait of character is their trump card in the competitive game of life. But they are not necessarily ambitious people, for their needs or objectives in life are usually quite simple; providing they maintain a certain standard of living, they are often content to sit back and let the world go by.

Their weak point of character can be this kind of inertia or lack of motivation, and this sudden swing or lack of enthusiasm is a serious undermining feature. Vine people must learn both to sow and to reap the harvest of life; nothing can be gained by one action alone. Successful vine characters are, however, the best examples of what can be achieved, and often against all the odds.

Love Life

In personal relationships their passionate nature lets off steam more openly. This may be due to a sense of personal frustration on occasions, for there is much to be resolved. Marriage is a difficult relationship to sustain, and vine people are perhaps the least married sign of the Celtic lunar zodiac. Much will depend on the choice of partner. The emotions and feelings of the Venusian character are not always easy to control, and represent the passions, the intense kind of emotions, of love or hate. There is also a very earthy quality associated with vine characters that some people find extremely sexy and sensual, but they can remain strangely aloof and project a very disinterested or indifferent response.

Summary

The changing cycles of life seldom run smoothly, but Vine people appear to experience a series of difficult adjustments from the very beginning of their lives. The most positive aspects to emerge are a great serenity of character and a calmness of spirit. Their sense of humor also swings to extremes; their laughter can so easily change to tears and vice versa. They are, generally, a refined people, who dislike coarse jokes or uncouth people. But there is another side to a Venusian character that can be both coarse and vulgar.

In the domestic scene these qualities change again, and their homes are usually well furnished, comfortable abodes. They like to live in scenic places, not too isolated but close to the amenities of the community. They enjoy the theater or cinema and generally patronize the arts, and some will have highly specialized musical talents.

They like shopping for their friends and family. There is a very feminine aspect to their nature, in both men and women, which promotes a great sensitivity. They can therefore be easily hurt or saddened by the lack of feeling in others. The mythology of Venus is well worth a study in understanding the feminine persona. There is a light and dark side that requires considerable balance or control, but if balance is found, vine people represent some of the finest examples of humanity.

CHAPTER ELEVEN

THE IVY

GORT

September 30 – October 27

Symbolizing: The Moon veiling Persephone
Gemstone: Opal
Flower: Woody nightshade
Archetypal Character: Arianrhod

"I am a ruthless boar"

The Illustration

The ivy is a climbing bush or shrub, but, unlike the vine, is an evergreen. A coverlet of ivy almost conceals the ruins of an ancient temple, and the tiny figures of the Sidhe dance wildly in the moonlight. The Sidhe, or faery people, were associated in Celtic mythology with the souls of the dead who awaited rebirth, and the atmosphere has a sense of both death and resurrection. The butterfly is a symbol of the Sidhe and symbolizes this metamorphic transition.

The Sidhe are often depicted riding on butterflies to remind us of this transformation aspect of the psyche. The astrological glyph of Persephone is part of the design of a butterfly's wing.

The bright red berries of the woody nightshade provide a late feast for the golden crested wren, a sacred Druidic bird, also hidden within the folds of the trailing ivy. The star cluster of the Pleiades makes a stunning reappearance as it symbolically rises to mark an important astronomical factor linked to a future eclipse.

The Opal

This stone has an almost unearthly loveliness, and yet its reputation for bad luck has caused it to be shunned around the world. The ancients, however, regarded the opal as a lucky stone, and the Asians referred to opals as the anchor of hope. The Arabians believed opals fell from the sky as a sign of heavenly joy.

How the stone came to have such ill repute is a mystery, but a belief regarding the opal as a bearer of bad luck began in Europe during the time of the Black Death; the luster of the opal is said to reflect the health of the wearer, and it had been observed at this time that it became brilliant at the point of death and then lost its luster completely. As a result the stone was thought to have caused the death, but the sudden change of body temperature associated with the plague, from fever (hot) to death (cold), would have affected the opal, which is slightly porous.

Although it is still considered a symbol of inconstancy, the Druids also believed it was a symbol of hope.

The Stone Temple

The Men-an-Tol stone in Cornwall is believed to be the solitary survivor of a destroyed tomb or temple built by the Megalithic people, the builders of Stonehenge, who inhabited the British Isles before the Celts. The Druids continued to use the same sites, and obviously understood the significance of the ancient stones; they carved their own symbols on some of the stones, and then began erecting their own standing stones inscribed with Ogham. The skill of working with stone continued to develop through the new religion of Christianity, and many ancient markstones following ley lines were roughly transformed to resemble a cross. The new faith gradually evolved its own identity, with ornately carved Celtic crosses appearing in the hundreds, as if to challenge the power of the silent stone giants.

There are still, however, numerous stone circles and huge granite boulders arranged in groups

known as cromlechs or dolmens, all over Britain, Ireland, and Brittany. The cromlechs are the remains of ancient burial chambers, while the stone circles had astronomical and ceremonial purposes. Holed stones have been linked to fertility rites, but the Men-an-Tol stone had another more mysterious feature.

According to ancient legends, all the stones were aligned with the powerful currents passing through the Earth, and with holed stones such as the Men-an-Tol the hole was the focus of this power. A healing force of renewed vitality was said to pass into the body of anyone who climbed through the hole. This energizing force has a psychic content according to local people, and it is said that if two brass pins are placed on the top of the stone they will mysteriously move or respond to answer any questions.

The Men-an-Tol stone faces west-east and is also reputedly on the same alignment or ley line as the chapel on Logan Rock at Bosiggran Castle, which has associations with the medieval Knights of St. John. Nearby is yet another circle of standing stones known as the Nine Maidens.

Knowledge of the harmonious use of the Earth energies has a universal following. The natural philosophy and religion of the ancient Greeks was inspired by their observance of nature; they saw a living spirit in every stone, in every tree, and in water the lovely shapes and figures of the naiads and satyrs. In China the science of natural energies is still keenly observed; it has a legal status and is known as *Feng shui,* which translates to "wind and water." The Chinese see a golden chain of spiritual life running through every form of creation. Their dragon men, who are the exponents of the ancient art and science of *Feng shui,* use their skills to determine the sites for all buildings and the tombs of their ancestors.

This reverence for natural energy and the elements was recognized by the Druids, who also related such energies to dragon or serpent symbolism. Their symbol of the ram-snake with spiral horns was associated with Cernunnos, a horned deity and a potent god of nature. Dragon energy relates to the ley lines that mark particular routes, but the Druids also spoke of the *wouivres* as channels of invisible energies that flowed through the surface of the Earth and crossed in special places. These special places were naturally considered holy sites, and the channels are also referred to in some legends as faery paths.

Faery People

References to faeries in European folklore form a vast amount of literature, and in the Celtic regions it represents a cultural heritage that is jealously preserved. In Ireland, a land where the Daoine Maithe or the good people still command a respectful nod, anyone foolish enough to build a house in the middle of a faery track is asking for trouble. The doors and windows on the front and back of the house cannot be locked or kept closed, but must remain open for the faeries to march through. This right of way is no mere fanciful superstition, but relates to the whole dimensional aspect of the faeries.

The faeries represent a time warp of ancestral memories that became identified with the psychic phenomenon of phantoms, ghosts, second sight, and all the unexplained things that go bump in the night—now including sightings of UFOs. Faery people, or the Sidhe (pronounced shee), in Irish Celtic mythology formed an integrating link with their ancient gods, the Tuatha Danaans, a race of immortals who lived in Ireland and Britain before the arrival of the Celts.

The Celts, who were known as the Milesians, invaded Ireland around 1015 B.C., according to Joyce, and displaced the Dannans after a fierce battle. But they did not force the Danaans to disperse or leave the land they loved. Instead, the Danaans employed their magical arts of invisibility to withdraw into their elaborate earth mounds or faery hills, and remained a source of ancient wisdom, mythical talents and music. What may have really occurred was that the Danaans were overwhelmed by the strength and numbers of the Celtic invaders, and withdrew into their underground hill forts to avoid further confrontations.

The Celts were not disposed to destroy a race of people who clearly fascinated them, and there followed a whole saga of legends that suggests a gradual intermingling of both blood and religion. With time, the ancient hill forts became deserted and the remaining Danaans either died out or drifted into Celtic society in the guise of gifted minstrels and bards. The Sidhe resembled humans in every physical respect, but they were all extremely beautiful and gifted people who did not die naturally, and derived their powers from enchantment or sorcery. This immortal quality cast a veil of mystery and magic over their own origins; in the Arthurian sagas they can be identified as the ladies of the lake, Merlin and Morgan le Fay.

The memory of their culture in later years was kept alive by faery faith, as it has been called, and subsequently came to cover a wide range of customs and beliefs. In some Irish myths there existed a more malevolent type of faery, the descendants of the Formorians, a race of deformed giants who had earlier been defeated by the Partholan people, but who remained beyond the northern seas and continued to harass the people of Ireland. This appears to explain the initial division into good faeries and bad faeries, but there are also environmental influences that appear to affect the behavior and ethnology of the faery people.

The Cornish pixies and Irish leprechauns appear to be earth spirits or elementals with a mischievous sense of humor. In Wales a faery race known as the Tylwth Teg usually appear after dark, and are described as a good little people who are fond of singing and dancing. There are faery pipers in Scotland who conferred their magical powers of music on the pipers of certain clans; a rivalry existed between the MacArthurs and Macrimmons for supremacy in the musical art, with both claiming patronage of the faeries. The faeries in Scotland are also said to be very fierce and vindictive, especially the water kelpies, who were known to drown people.

The faeries are known by various names and deeds too numerous to mention in any great detail, but as harbingers of death they are known as corrigans in Brittany and banshees in Scotland and Ireland. This link with the dead relates to the underworld in Celtic mythology, a place where souls awaited rebirth. According to some legends, the faeries also came to represent the lost souls who could not reincarnate but remained earthbound

because of their rejection of human society with its narrow values and Christian religion.

The Butterfly

The butterfly became a symbol of this particular faery faith, and was worn as a brooch or badge by Celtic people as a mark of respect for their ancestral spirits. Whatever their original conception, the faeries have a mystique that challenges rational thinking and material world values.

The Woody Nightshade

The bright red berries of the woody nightshade are ripe in the month of the ivy, and add a splash of vibrant color to the autumn hedgerows. Woody nightshade is a native plant to Britain, and was known in the Middle Ages as *Amaradulcis,* meaning bittersweet, a name still used by country people for its taste. Old herbalists valued it highly, and used its narcotic properties for slowing the heart rate and lowering the temperature. The berries, however, like those of the deadly nightshade, are poisonous, and although they are not as dangerous or potentially fatal, they have proved poisonous to young children.

In the days when witchcraft was feared, shepherds hung the whole plant, with its berries, around the necks of their beasts to protect them from the evil eye, a custom that certainly relates back to the Druids, who used the berries as part of an antidote to more deadly poisons.

The Ivy

The ivy also has one species that is highly toxic and poisonous, not surprisingly known as poison ivy. Its leaves can cause a most uncomfortable rash, with the whole body becoming swollen simply by touching or handling the plant.

The common ivy is, by contrast, a luscious dark green hardy evergreen and has become a favorite ornamental creeping shrub for the garden; it is found over the greater part of Europe, and northern and central Asia. It has an ancient history and was held in esteem by the Greeks; Bacchus, their vine-god, to whom the plant was dedicated, wore a crown of ivy, the practice of wearing ivy leaves as a crown being to prevent the adverse effects of intoxication. An old remedy, also said to counter such ill effects, was made by gently boiling a handful of ivy leaves in wine and drinking the cooled mixture.

The ivy is the plant badge of the Gordons, who had their origins in the Lowlands of Scotland. They were then granted the lands of Huntly or Strathbogi by Bruce, and subsequently raised two famous regiments to form the Gordon Highlanders. The town of St. Ives in Cornwall has no authorized arms, but those attributed to the town incorporated an ivy branch. The ivy bush has always been the sign of a wine tavern in England, and ivy ale was a highly intoxicating medieval drink, still reputedly brewed at Trinity College, Oxford, in memory of a Trinity student murdered by Balliol men.

The medicinal virtues of the ivy are little used today by modern herbalists, but the older practitioners, Gerard and Culpeper, rated it more highly and used it for a number of ailments. They both mention in particular the ground ivy for use internally, for easing griping pains, and for windy, choleric humors in the stomach and spleen. It also cleansed ulcerated lungs and other parts internally, and, externally, healed wounds, sores, and cankers.

The Druids left a legacy of herbal remedies still remembered in Ireland today. Irish country people will tell you to chew the leaves of ground ivy to clear the chest of any congestion. The juice of the leaves is also used to cure wounds, ulcers, burns, scalds, and stuffed in the nose to purge the head of slimy colds. A cure for a soft corn is to tie an ivy leaf around it, but if this is not successful, a handful of ivy leaves steeped in vinegar, tightly corked for forty-eight hours and then applied carefully is guaranteed to work.

The Druids and Greek priests presented newly married couples with a wreath of ivy to confer a blessing of strength and eternal love on the union. A crown of ivy was presented to the winners of the first Eisteddfods or annual festivals of the arts held by the bardic orders. During the eleventh lunar month the ivy was in its flowering season, and was used to decorate the sacred shrines and altars of the Druids, the evergreen aspect of the ivy representing the immortality of the spirit, just as the faery people came to represent a residue of their nature.

Gort

Gort relates to the Greek word *gortys,* the name of the reputed founder of Gortys, a city in southern Arcadia. Gortyns is the name of a famous town in Crete and is believed to represent a title of a goddess—Gorgopa or "fearful-faced," an epithet of the death goddess Athene. This link or association is an appropriate one, considering the symbolism associated with the month of the ivy.

Lunar Symbolism Relating to Persephone

In the Egyptian pantheon of gods, this sign is symbolically linked to Isis' twin sister Nephthys, the hidden or dark aspect of spirit. Isis was consort to Osiris, and their relationship in Egyptian myth follows a very similar annual cycle of birth, death, and rebirth through the aid of magic to that of the Celtic ritual year. Nephthys was also the wife of Set, the dark twin of Osiris, whose symbol was the black boar (waning Moon) that devours the white boar (waxing Moon) in a primitive Egyptian lunar myth explaining the original battle of the gods—the conflict between good and evil. This association certainly explains the Druids' incantation "I am a ruthless boar" as darkness begins to overwhelm light in the Celtic lunar calendar, and once again reveals another ancient link between the Egyptians and the Celts.

Astrological Significance

The astrological rulership is partly designated to the Moon, for in esoteric astrology the Sun and Moon are said to veil or eclipse hidden planets. The Moon in the month of the ivy is therefore veiling a hidden planet yet to be discovered, and which, according to the ancients, lies on the other side of Pluto. The name of Persephone has been chosen because of the evidence for this planet, which has long been considered by astronomers a suspected planet—either a dual planet with Pluto or possibly a satellite or Moon within the gravitational orbit of Pluto.

This choice of name is not by chance, but fits into the mythological cycle of the planets in our universe. In Greek mythology Persephone, daughter of Ceres or Gaia, the great Earth mother goddess, was kidnapped by Pluto, god of the underworld, and forced to remain with him for six months of the year. Persephone was also a lunar goddess, and identified with Hecate in the transformation aspect of their triple goddess. The astrological interpretation is further explained in the next section.

Archetypal Character

In Celtic myth Persephone and Nephthys can be identified with the lunar goddesses Arianrhod or Rhiannon. Both these Celtic deities have an ancient association with rebirth and the mysterious rites connected with the female, and both endured a forced exile or penance that temporarily displaced them. Arianrhod had, however, a more mysterious or hidden nature, and is therefore the archetypal character associated with this sign. The mythology of the faery people also provides an insight into these elusive personal qualities.

But the mythology of the ivy relating to immortality symbolizes the fundamental energies associated with the month of the ivy in the Druidic calendar. As the Sun remains low on the horizon, the spectacular sunsets symbolize a transformation rather than a permanent change. It is a time, however, when a certain endurance and stamina are necessary in order to survive the coming winter and prevailing forces of darkness.

Tree Character

Ivy characters have a personal stamina, second to none. People born under this sign are also blessed with abundant talents that can bring personal honors and public recognition. They usually remain modest but colorful individuals with a unique style of their own. They have a sharp intellect and make amusing witty mimics.

There is a serious side to their nature, however, which has a quiet faith in natural justice. Their own doubts and fears can manifest in the form of strange dreams and personal encounters, just as darkness is drawn to light. For that reason hope is attributed to this sign, to combat the darker element of the psyche.

Some notable ivy characters are Oscar Wilde, Lillie Langtry, Sarah Bernhardt, Mahatma Gandhi, and Margaret Thatcher.

Positive Aspects

These include their loyalty to colleagues and friends, and their ability to accept full responsibility for their own actions. They are generous providers, but also thrifty savers or investors regarding the future security of their families.

Negative Aspects

They are extremely manipulative people who will use their position or influence quite ruthlessly. They tend to attract the unstable energies of life, and people of baser instincts, as they try to establish their own code of morality—or immorality. Ivy characters hold the power of justice in the symbolic sense, but in human terms they often become involved in acrimonious legal disputes and litigations.

General

Their true talents are rarely learned from books or the accepted method of training; in fact they often make poor students in the conventional sense, and prefer to use their own ideas in all areas of work. They are quite radical thinkers, akin to the rowan tree characters, but have more artistic flair. People born under this sign have a pronounced artistic temperament generally, with a conflict of material values not unlike the ash tree characters.

However, ivy people are more shrewd with regard to the saving of money or the investment of finances, because of their overwhelming need for future security. The future often holds a kind of dread for them, although they may never willingly admit to such fears or apprehensions. Indeed, their fortunes appear to swing between two extremes, from relative obscurity to sudden fame, then back again, and will set the pattern of life accordingly. But there is an element of luck that appears to follow them throughout their life, as if the "little people" are watching over them. Ivy people are quite psychic themselves and may have inherited the divinatory powers known as faery gifts.

Love Life

Personal relationships are the most sensitive and highly emotive areas of life for most people. But for the ivy people there is an extreme reaction of falling in and out of love; of being in love one day, then suddenly, because of the need for freedom, severing the relationship with a sharp sword, as if to make certain there is no time for regrets of any kind. And there is another equally extreme reaction of being overly possessive, of clinging, like the creeping ivy that tends to overwhelm other plant life; the worst aspect of this trait is not recognizing when a relationship is over.

Ivy characters are generous, caring parents when they are around, but they are often missing during the important early years, due to their careers and personal ambitions. This can also affect their personal relationships and marriage partners and, perhaps unwittingly, creates the very instability they strive so hard to avoid. If this point is acknowledged and their personal extremes reconciled at some stage, they have a greater chance than most of finding a perfect match and a truly harmonious relationship.

Summary

Ivy characters hate indecision, and in their careers they are often impelled to make a great number of choices or decisions that require a firm commitment. They are naturally enterprising people and have the potential for most careers or professions. All their personal skills have creative direction and practical application. Diplomacy is one of their best personal skills, although they may never develop the art of compromise.

People value their friendship, and they have a circle of friends across the globe, for they travel widely to strange and remote places—seeking out the unknown is part of their approach to life, for they are very curious people. They are also a very humorous people, their sense of humor often being quite outrageous and spontaneous, making other people laugh at themselves or their own misfortunes.

They prefer to live in high places—penthouses or houses perched on top of steep hills. This is because they feel uneasy in places surrounded by too many trees or in deep hollows. Large windows to let in the light are also an important feature.

Their lifestyle makes other people envious, in the sense that they seem to create a perfect scenario. Ivy people use the same magic as the willow people to effect illusions, but they are nevertheless extremely believable illusions.

CHAPTER TWELVE
THE REED

NGETAL

October 28 – November 24

Symbolizing: *The planet Pluto*
Gemstone: *Jasper*
Flower: *Watermint*
Archetypal Character: *Pwyll, head of Annwn*

"I am a threatening noise of the sea"

The Illustration

The reed grows wild on a river bank and has a dense growth of slender form. A north wind chills the air as a flock of geese passes overhead on their homeward journey.

The Celtic festival of Samhain was a time when doors were opened between the natural and supernatural world. The divisionary line is symbolically overshadowed with the dark blue river that flows into the subterranean cavern where Pluto, god of the underworld, rules with a melancholy air. Pluto or Dis was the guardian of the four treasures that the Celts had inherited from the Tuatha Danaans, a race of immortals who became their gods.

Samhain not only marked the beginning of the Celtic New Year in the ritual calendar of the Celts, but it also officially marked the beginning of winter in their seasonal calendar. The celebration of Samhain on the first day of November lasted three days in the ritual calendar, and it was the most important festival of the whole year.

Jasper

There are many different color variations of jasper, ranging from green to black. The red variety, the bloodstone, is particularly suitable for this sign, but all shades are equally acceptable and express the magical property of the stone.

The bloodstone was regarded as a powerful protective amulet in ancient Egypt, where it represented the blood of Isis. Throughout history it has been associated with blood and bleeding; for example, the Babylonian magicians used it in the treatment of blood disorders, and to stop internal bleeding. The Gnostics used it extensively and made an amulet from the stone called heliotrope; it reputedly made the wearer invisible, a belief referred to by Dante in the *Inferno*.

A black variety of jasper known as the Lydian Stone was the touchstone of the ancient alchemists, and was used to test gold. The connection with gold is a relevant association, as the gods of the underworld were considered the wealthiest gods, for they owned all the mines. The Druids believed it had a power over the Sun itself, and could cause storms and tempests.

Samhain

All Celtic feasts began on the eve of the celebrated day, for they calculated their days from sunset to sunrise in the lunar tradition. Bearing this in mind, the ritual calendar thus began when the Sun was setting in the ecliptic system—a system used by all ancient astronomer-priests, including the Druids, to determine the seasons by the Sun's movement. The eve of Samhain was one of the great spirit nights of the Celtic people, the other being the eve of Beltane in May. This was a time when the boundaries between the natural and supernatural worlds dissolved. Consequently, it was a night for divination and prophecy.

Samhain was a festival of the dead—the past dead, the past year, and the end of a complete cycle on the Celtic wheel of life. It was also a time of purification, with the burning of effigies that symbolized the terrors of the past, and all that troubled a

fearful mind. The Samhain bonfire ritually burned the ashes of the old year and, through this purification, the people were then able to face the rigors of the dark winter months that lay ahead. The ashes were then scattered on the land in the saining rite that followed.

In Celtic mythology the faery people or the Sidhe also celebrated Samhain; indeed, they appeared to be the rulers of the Feast of the Dead. On November eve the faeries could take mortal husbands, and all the faery hills were opened to allow any mortal bold enough to take a look into their realm and admire their palaces full of treasures. But few Celts ever willingly ventured into their enchanted kingdom; their respect for the faeries was one of awe, tinged with a sense of dread.

In Brittany on November eve, or La Toussaint, the custom of leaving a place at the table for the dead was more than a sign of respect. The Breton Celt made no distinction between the living and the dead; both were believed to inhabit this world, one being visible, the other invisible. In Celtic Ireland, Oidhche Shamhna, or November eve, heralded the start of great feasting, with games and races in honor of Tlachtga, an ancient mother goddess. From this most ancient deity, the Cailleach and the Morrigan were later drawn. The Cailleach thus came to preside over this festival and celebrated the event with a symbolic coupling with the Dagda, another ancient deity and a god of *draidecth,* the founder of Druidism. They both represented the ancient primeval forces responsible for death and rebirth.

The Celts stubbornly retained their ancient festivals by incorporating them into Christian celebrations. The last day of October thus became known as All Hallow's Eve or All Saints Night, more popularly known as Halloween. In later years the spirit of Samhain again reappeared as Guy Fawkes Night in Britain, with many of the old customs still being observed, and is now celebrated on November 5 with huge bonfires and firework displays around the country.

Watermint

The wild growing watermint was a favorite Druidic herb, and is one of the commonest mints. It grows abundantly in wet places, on river banks and marshes, and is identified by its whorls of lilac or purple flowers. The scent is strong and unpleasant, but its properties yield some valuable herbal remedies. Culpeper used it for a variety of ailments.

All mints make a good base for herbal tisanes or, if steeped in wine and sipped, will ease wind and colic and stomach dyspepsia. The Druids used it for similar cures, and as a simple but effective head purge by stuffing it up the nose.

The Reed

The reed belongs to a family or genus of widely distributed tall grasses only found in wet places, from North Africa to the continent of Asia. Its dense growth has a thick root, like a tree, which is perhaps why the Celts identified it with a submerged or hidden *dryad,* an association that is also a clear reference to Dis, their god of the underworld. The festival of the dead may have been presided over by the faeries and the Cailleach, but the underworld realm belonged to Dis or Pluto.

The mythology relating to the twelfth month of the reed is both ancient and singular, the reed being perhaps the most curious of symbols in the Celtic zodiac. From ancient times the reed was a symbol of royalty and was associated with the number twelve in the eastern Mediterranean. The Egyptian pharaohs used reed scepters, and a royal reed was said to have been put in Jesus' hand when he was attired in scarlet before the Crucifixion. The number twelve to the ancient Hebrews was the sign of established power, and the word *reed* is an archaic word for "arrow." The Irish Celts associated both with their Sun-god Lugh, who was said to fire reed arrows to proclaim his sovereignty and to disperse his enemies. Reed arrows were considered the swiftest flying arrow shafts, the hollow stalk sometimes being filled with poisonous substances to make them truly deadly missiles.

But during the twelfth month of the lunar calendar the more practical uses of the reed were utilized. At this time the reed became ready for cutting, and was used by the Celts for thatching their houses. The reed month was recorded in Celtic literature as a time when the roar of sea and the snarling east winds whistled dismally through the reed beds of the rivers. In Ireland the roaring of the sea and the harsh cry of the screech owl was held to be a prophetic sign of a king's death. The screech owl was also identified with the unfaithful wife of their Sun-god Lugh or Lleu, and during the moonlit nights of November the owl is always at its most vocal. A reference is remembered in the ancient folklore of Ireland, whereby reeds were picked just before sunrise and strewn in the bedroom by husbands who suspected their wives of adultery. The reeds apparently had the power to drive the adultress mad and force her to confess her erring ways.

The reed or bulrush is the plant badge of the Scottish clan names of Innes, Mackay, and Sutherland. In heraldry the reed occurs on the crest of the Reades, and that of the Middlemores; it also occurs on the crest of Billiat and the arms of Scott.

Ngetal

Ngetal is the Ogham name for the reed, but there are other Gaelic names relating to the reed, such as *gaothaiche,* which means "hollow" and relates to the mouthpiece of a bagpipe. The pipes of the bagpipe were originally made from reeds and, according to Celtic legend, were first invented and supplied by the faeries. There are many legends and stories concerning the music of the faery pipers, who passed on the art to some favored mortals. The haunting music of the pipes cannot fail to stir the blood of a Celt, no matter how widely scattered their seed.

Plutonian Symbolism

The underworld was conceived by the Celts as a place of primal creative power, and not a place of punishment. It was a place where souls resided while awaiting rebirth, with death being part of a transformation process of the soul in the Druidic religion. Annwfn or Annwn was another name for the astral plane within the underworld, a place or dimension where mortals and the gods of the underworld could enter into a special relationship. There are several underworld deities mentioned in Celtic mythology, but perhaps the most interesting myth concerns Arawn, King of Annwn of the underworld regions, and Pwyll, Lord of Dyfed. Its symbolism relates to the dual identity or nature of man and the battle for supremacy between the powers of light and darkness, or the higher and lower self.

The story begins with Pwyll, who is out hunting and becomes separated from his companions. A strange pack of white hounds crosses his path and attempts to bring down a stag. Pwyll drives off the hounds and sets his own hounds on the quarry and they eventually bring down the stag. But Pwyll is then suddenly confronted with another hunter, the owner of the white hounds, who rebukes him for his discourtesy. The stranger then introduces himself as Arawn, King of Annwn (the underworld), and Pwyll realizes that he must come to terms with this great ruler.

In order to redeem himself, Pwyll agrees to change places with Arawn for a year and a day, and live in the underworld regions. At the end of the year he must also meet Arawn's enemy, Hafgan, another underworld ruler, and defeat him in a contest at the ford that divides the underworld regions from the visible world. Arawn tells Pwyll that he must on no account strike Hafgan twice, for the second blow would restore his power. They exchange forms, and Pwyll descends into the underworld, where he finds that Arawn's wife accepts him quite naturally, not knowing of the deception. But Pwyll observes a strict code of chastity with the queen, and in due course defeats Hafgan, and so becomes the sole King of Annwn. When Arawn returns he is delighted with the conduct of Pwyll, and they forge a firm bond of friendship. Pwyll, as a result of his stay in Annwn, has united the two kingdoms and was henceforth known as Pwyll, the Head of Annwn.

The significance of this myth in symbolic terms reveals the intense drama that is always associated with the purging aspect of Pluto.

Myths Associated with the Sign

In the book *Mythologies* by Yeats, the journey of Red Hanrahan provides an original insight into the Celtic mysteries, and is a direct comparison with Sir Percival who seeks the Grail in the Arthurian legend. The young Celtic warrior finds his own destiny when he goes in search of adventure.

On the eve of Samhain, Red Hanrahan becomes lost in a strange country known as Slieve Echtge (a faery realm) and sits down to rest while he tries to find his bearings. After a little while he notices a strange doorway in the hillside, with a bright light streaming under the door. He is naturally curious, and opens the door to find himself in a huge space filled with a light brighter than day. He appears to be outside a grand house, where he meets an old man who is gathering summer thyme and yellow flag flowers. All the sweet smells of summer drift around him. As he steps farther inside, the light becomes brighter, with every color of nature shining like a rainbow.

Presently he discovers a room filled with all the most wonderful treasures known to man. At the end of the room the most beautiful woman in the world sits on a high throne, but she has the tired look of one who has been waiting a long time. Sitting below her, four silver-haired old women hold the four great treasures of the Celtic people: one holds the cauldron of the Dagda in her lap; another has the Lia Fail upon her knees; the third holds the hugh spear of Finias; and the last old woman holds the invincible sword of Lugh without a scabbard. The first old woman stands up and, holding the cauldron between her hands, mutters "Pleasure." Then the second one rises and, holding the stone in her hands, whispers "Power," and the third old woman rises with the spear in her hands and cries loudly, "Courage." Finally the last of the old women rises with the sword in her hands and says slyly "Knowledge." Then the four old women walk slowly out the door carrying with them the four treasures.

This particular myth contains the seeds of great truths, and the whole saga has the uncanny links with time that appear to govern the spiritual experiences of the Celts. The ability to move in and out of time certainly dominated the early Druidic religion, and remained evident long after their conversion to Christianity.

Astrological Significance

The astrological significance of the month of the reed is clearly defined with the festival of Samhain, the festival of the dead. The planet Pluto is the designated ruler of this sign, its mythology and astrological interpretation having all the corresponding associations with the Celtic cult of the dead; also known as the cult of the underworld, this was the source or central belief from which the Druidic religion evolved. All Celts claimed descent from Dis, or Pluto, the god of the underworld, the administrator of the chthonic power that lies deeply buried within the human psyche.

In esoteric astrology, Pluto brings change through darkness and death, the destructive power of death signifying the death of desire and the death of the personality. However Pluto or death can never destroy the conscious aspect or spirit, this being clearly defined in the Celtic myth of Pwyll. Pluto or Pwyll basically relate to the regenerative powers of the human psyche and, in more personal terms, to a character who can develop immense power for both good and evil. But there is also a healing aspect related to Pluto, which is often overlooked; psychologically it prunes dead wood and cauterizes festering wounds with surgical precision.

Archetypal Character

The archetypal character associated with the sign of the reed is Pwyll, the Celtic Pluto, who represents the interplay of both light and darkness, or the struggle between the higher and lower self. Like the ivy character, there is great emphasis on personal mortality, and this interplay seeks to establish or redefine the boundaries.

But there is a subtle difference; the ivy character, symbolized by Persephone, represents the feminine anima in the development of the personality, while Pluto represents the animus. In Jungian psychology the anima is related to the unconscious feelings that appear purposeless and can remain fantasies. The Pluto animus is related to the consciousness, or persona, although both terms have a psychological bisexuality found in men and women. According to Jung, the anima and animus are seen as the bridge or door leading to the collective unconscious, just as the persona is the bridge into the world. Ivy people are therefore drawn into a spiritual recess or niche, while reed people experience a spiritual revelation, both being evolutionary processes.

Tree Character

Reed characters have a powerful presence or personal magnetism that can both attract and overpower sensitive people. People born under this sign are something of a mystery to family and friends alike. Their personal achievements or success can also suddenly rise or fall overnight, like those of the vine and ivy people, but they never lack purpose and the personal ability to overcome impossible odds. However, in order to maintain their position, the virtue of justice, the moral principle of fair play, must be their guiding light, for if they stray off this narrow marker chaos and darkness will reign supreme.

Some notable reed characters are Cleopatra, Voltaire, King Edward VII of Great Britain, and Madame Curie.

Positive Aspects

These include their sense of purpose and their subtle persistence. They are also highly imaginative, and possess a clear vision or insight into the complexities of life. They make powerful friends and allies. Their business acumen reveals a formidable strength of character.

Negative Aspects

They can become insanely jealous people, resentful of other people's success, their powerful feelings and emotions becoming distorted into jealous rages and violent anger. They may also become involved in illegal transactions or profits.

General

The uncompromising statement in the introductory paragraph to this section is perhaps the best way to tackle the personal potential that is trying to reestablish itself. However, reed characters are also naturally secretive, and, like the ivy people, will not openly admit to any fears or feelings of inadequacy. There is a basic duality in all people, but in this sign it takes the form of a struggle for power or dominance that is nor easily controlled.

Reed people therefore strive for complete power, not only within themselves, but also endeavoring to influence others during the process. They may do this totally unconsciously to begin with, by the very strength of their personality, but later they will begin to understand and perhaps enjoy what this influence can bring. Those who are aware of it, however, will constantly resort to putting themselves down or refusing to get involved in personal power games, knowing too well the consequences.

The choice of career is not easily decided on initially, and can follow a series of flops or disappointments. This is primarily due to a basic immaturity, but this will suddenly be replaced by a ruthlessness or cunning that doesn't appear very pleasant; it is, however, the upsurge of a powerful survival instinct that at first may have a rather raw edge.

The cut and thrust of the business world may attract, or any avenue in which personal drive and creativity is required for research or investigation. Reed people make good leaders because of their fearless attitudes, but few people are brave enough to

stay in the firing line with them. Dangerous occupations may become their forte, but the underlying point of issue is their overwhelming need to break free from all restrictions, which may initially be linked to the dominant influence of a parent or foster parent. This particular aspect is often shown when they work hard to build up a career and then, for reasons best known to themselves, destroy their work or what it represents and disappear from the scene, to start again somewhere else.

They are also subject to overwhelming external pressures and to the larger dimension of life called fate. Of all the signs, reed people are the most "fated," something that could be termed either good or bad, depending on one's perspective.

Love Life

Reed characters are passionate people, inclined to jealousy and suspicion, the fact of the matter being that they enjoy the intrigue more than anything else. But on a more positive note, anyone brave enough to get involved with reed characters will find that they are immensely caring people and highly imaginative lovers. Indeed, they make very persistent lovers, even if it is hate at first sight. They are very subtle and determined people.

But marriage or personal relationships are difficult to maintain at times because of the intense emotions involved. Lasting friendships are also difficult to keep going, and are not usually intimate in any sense. Although there may be the odd relationship or friendship that will last, this will be a strange affair; it may involve no intimate or close contact, but will prompt great loyalty and affection.

Summary

Their determination often has an inflexible quality and, as parents, they can be overly authoritative. They will not extend any favors to their children unless they feel they have earned them. Their children are, however, loved deeply for themselves, no matter their faults or shortcomings. Not surprisingly, therefore, there is a capacity within all reed characters to love the Devil himself—a strange statement, but it does explain the nature of the reed people, who are capable of overcoming the powers of darkness or dangerous adversaries by using their own highly developed instincts or psychic abilities.

Their life pattern is a series of dramatic adjustments to life rather than normal transitions, and more disruptive than those experienced by the alder and vine characters. It may mean several residences in a short space of time, but they will finally settle in the most unlikely places and adopt a very conventional lifestyle. They are extremely hardy people, and can endure harsh conditions that would defeat everyone else, even the ivy people. This capacity or will power has tremendous influence on people who cross their path, but they remain the most enigmatic characters of the Celtic lunar zodiac.

CHAPTER THIRTEEN

THE ELDER TREE

RUIS

November 25 – December 22

Symbolizing:	*The planet Saturn*
Gemstone:	*Jet*
Flower:	*Dandelion*
Archetypal Character:	*Pryderi, son of Pwyll*

"I am a wave of the sea"

THE NAMELESS DAY

December 23

Gemstone:	*The black pearl*
Plant:	*The mistletoe*

"Who but I know the secrets of the unhewn dolmen?"

The Illustration

The elder is a bushy tree with a dark green foliage and clusters of purple-black berries. Although not in blossom at this time of year, the symbolism of its magical berries relates to inception, the beginning of the mystical birth of the Celtic Sun-god. The tree in dark shadow form is growing within the doorway of Newgrange, an ancient Celtic earth tomb, with its strangely carved entrance stones on either side. A huge black raven, its wings spanning the entrance, is caught in the brilliant light coming from inside the tomb. The bird has a wreath of mistletoe around its neck and is carrying in its sharp beak a lustrous black pearl. Its racous cry disturbs the scene as a messenger of impending death, the physical death that precedes a spiritual rebirth.

The Earth at this time is in darkness as the psyche struggles toward the light. The dazzling gold petals and frosted white seeds of the dandelion symbolize the dual light of the solar spirit as it regenerates the sleeping ancestral spirits of the Celts. The secret of Annwn, the Celtic underworld, is revealed at the time of the winter solstice, which marks the shortest day and heralds the rebirth of the Sun.

Jet

Jet, sometimes referred to as black amber, has been used as an amulet since prehistoric times. It is a hard black variety of lignite, and was extensively mined at Whitby on the coast of Yorkshire in the British Isles from the time of the Bronze Age. Jet has also been found in the ruins of ancient cities in Mesopotamia, in Bronze Age burial sites, and was mined by the Romans and the Vikings, the latter engraving their runic inscriptions upon the stone.

There is little doubt that the main value of jet lay in its reputed magical properties. The magicians of Saxon England used jet in their sorceries for conferring wishes or desires, a point remarked upon by the Venerable Bede, who preferred to mention its healing properties. The Druids believed that, when burned, the fumes of jet had a number of magical powers, including the expulsion of demons.

The Winter Solstice

The winter solstice on December 22 was known as Alban Arthuan in the Druidic calendar—a time when the Sun appeared to stand still, having reached its most southerly point. It marked a turning point in the relationship between the Sun and Earth, a dividing line after which the Sun would henceforth begin its ascent in the sky.

But it was the sunset on December 20 that signaled the death of the old Sun, as it appeared to fall into the sea at St. David's Head in Wales. The pale golden Sun rising on the day before the winter solstice was regarded as the shadow of the Sun, or the dual aspect that was really a false Sun. The true Sun was a prisoner of Arawn, King of Annwn, the Celtic underworld. The Druids also believed that when the Sun was reborn on December 22 as a babe of Ceridwen, myriads of lives apart from the physical existence would emanate at the same time.

However, the Druids did not worship the Sun or the Moon. The Druidic trinity represented three rays

of their great creator Celi, which became identified with the Sun, Moon, and Earth in their bilinear matrix or system of evolution. The Druids fervently believed that, in some inconceivably distant era, the active principle of Celi had concentrated its energy into the passive principle of Ced or Ceridwen, and as a result the Sun was created.

The Sun, nevertheless, was regarded as a primeval agent or power, and under its influence the atomic elements took solid shape and became an embryonic chaos known as Calen. The substance of Calen had a primitive numerical formula, from whence evolved a system of reckoning—the calendar. The Celtic lunar calendar of a 28-day month with one intercalary day is frequently referred to in the myths and ancient poems of the Celts, and predates the Gaulish Coligny calendar (first century B.C.) with its suspect Romanized abbreviations. Robert Graves, in his book *The White Goddess,* was of the opinion that the bronze tablet engraved with Roman abbreviations and unearthed at Coligny, northeast of Lyon, in France (1897) cannot be interpreted with any certainty, and was not of Druidic origin, but merely an attempt by the Romans under Claudius to Romanize the Celts—a view shared by other eminent scholars of such antiquities. Reference to the intercalated days recorded by the Coligny Calendar survive in Welsh folklore, but in both Irish and Welsh myths of more ancient pedigree there are constant references to the *Beth-Luis-Nion* calendar of 364 days plus one (derived from thirteen 28-day months).

To confirm this point, the Celts tended to personify their kings or solar deities as the calendar year and their first-born son as personification of the extra day. In the Irish myth of King Conchobar, he was thus personified, and in another myth relating to the wooing of Elmer the Celtic hero Cuchulain was opposed by the lady's father, whose name was Calatin. Calatin, with his twenty-seven sons and one grandson, insisted on being regarded as a single warrior, claiming that all his offspring were constituent parts of his own body. The twenty-eight parts were a symbolic reference to the lunar month and the need to overcome time, a belief shared by many classic civilizations.

Newgrange

The Cult of the Dead was reputed to be the religion of the Megalithic people (4000-3000 B.C.) who built the portal dolmens and cromlechs, and the stone circles throughout Britain, Ireland, and Europe. The most famous and significant Megalithic sites are Stonehenge in Britain, Carnac in Brittany, and Newgrange in Ireland. But the building of Newgrange in Ireland, which has been undergoing recent extensive renovations and rebuilding, may soon be regarded as the eighth wonder of the world—on a par with the Great Pyramid and the ancient Greek edifices. The other equally imposing earth mounds of Koweth, a few miles from Newgrange, are only now being examined by a team of experts to determine their true age, although it is already believed to be around 5000 B.C. This would predate the Great Pyramid and many other ancient wonders relating to the Old World civilizations.

Yet there is an interlinking relationship between Stonehenge and Newgrange that has a much wider plan and dimension when envisaged on a cosmic scale, for they represent the two spiritual centers of

life and death, the dual reality of all existence. The midsummer phenomenon of the Sun at Stonehenge places the Sun at its zenith, and is a parallel or polarity with the winter phenomenon of the Sun at Newgrange, when the dying Sun dramatically illuminates the inner chamber of the Newgrange tomb. In fact this occurs on a number of days surrounding the winter solstice, when spectacular solar light was apparently visualized as an energizing force that regenerated the spirits of the Celtic dead. This very relevant point provides the key to their belief in the immortality of their ancestral soul force or spiritual identity, which was also the source of their own spiritual and evolutionary process.

According to legend, both the kings of Tara and the Celtic Sun-god Lugh were buried at Newgrange. This confirms the continued usage of the tomb by the Druids, who obviously superimposed their own religion on to the structures already in place. Indeed, they may have recognized the Cult of the Dead as the pristine source of their own religion, and consequently realigned their own faith.

The entrance stone to Newgrange is carved with spiral symbols denoting the motion of the Sun as it appears to move in a spiral pathway around the Earth. Indeed Newgrange is famous for its many decorated stones; some are carved with lozenges, cup-and-ring marks and the larger, more ornate encompassing spirals that form labyrinths and mazes—the symbols of immortality—while other geometrical designs can be seen on the large kerb stones around the base of the mound, on the outside as well as inside the chambers. The elaborate construction of the mound required a number of differ-

ent types of stones, and is one of the finest examples of a passage grave in Europe. The superb outer circle of water-rolled cairn stones and dazzling white quartz stones appears to glow from a distance, and on dark moonlit winter nights projects an unearthly light in the sky.

The Celts had inherited a land of strange relics from a mysterious race of people, and it is therefore perhaps not surprising that they remained an intensely superstitious and psychically alert people. Second sight, or prophecy, is still considered a natural talent in Ireland and the Highlands of Scotland, where the rugged landscape and climate lends itself to sudden and dramatic changes that foster a brooding air of silent uncertainty.

The Black Raven

The black raven was a bird of death or ill omen to many ancient people, and was particularly meaningful both to the Gaels, and to the Cornish Celts, who to this day watch the sky for any dark flock of birds. In days long since past omen and augury formed an essential part of daily life for all Celts; the movement and nature of every living thing had an occult or hidden meaning, and the phenomena of the animal kingdom played an important role in the whole rhythm of life. To the Cornish Celt the chough was the most sacred bird, into whose body passed the soul of Arthur, their great king. To the Irish and Scottish Gaels it was the eagle, who talked with St. Patrick, that was sacred.

The Dandelion

This is a native plant to Greece. It thrives under almost any conditions and may be found in bloom throughout the year, and has consequently spread to nearly every part of the world. Its name is derived from the Greek words leon and tondron, meaning "lion" and "tooth," because of the resemblance of the jagged leaves to the teeth of a lion.

The lion is a solar symbol but, according to Culpeper, the plant comes under the dominion of Jupiter, due to its ability to cleanse the liver. It was also a favorite Romany herb for rheumatism, a remedy reputedly passed down from more ancient times. It was found in old Irish herbals with Druidic associations. The plant was considered a natural tonic, and is rich in vitamin C, calcium, and numerous other essential nutrients. Although the Druids obviously didn't know about vitamins or nutrients, they did understand that the plant had vital life-giving properties. This vital energy, plus the ability of the plant to protect itself from the heat of the Sun by closing its petals, indicated its endurance and the will to survive, which relates very well to the month of the elder.

The Elder

The elder tree has a history of folklore and legend, both from many European countries and from more distant continents. A strange mixture of romance and superstition engenders a mysterious aura over the small bushy tree.

The word elder comes from the Anglo-Saxon word aeld, meaning fire, the hollow stems being quite literally used for blowing up a fire. But the generic name of the elder, Sambucus, occurs in the writings of Pliny as being derived from the Greek Sambucu, associated with an ancient musical instrument; for the Greeks and Romans apparently fashioned a panpipe or flute from its hollow stems, and, from its hard wood, a stringed instrument.

But this is a tree also associated with witches, faeries, and devilry. It is a tree reputed to have provided the cross for the Crucifixion, and upon which Judas hanged himself. The elder-leaf shape of funerary flints found in Megalithic long-barrows certainly suggests a long-standing association with death. Not all associations with death are gloomy, however, and, although the elder wood was used for funeral purposes, it was also planted on new graves by the Welsh and Manx Celts; if it blossomed, the soul of the person beneath it was believed to be happy in the land of Tir-nan-oge, the land of youth—another, more romantic, name for the Celtic other world or heaven. Green branches of elder were also buried in a grave to protect the dead against witchcraft.

Russian peasants and the Bohemians believed that elder branches could drive away evil spirits, and the Serbs took an elder stick to weddings for good luck. In parts of England it has a more mixed history; Shakespeare referred to it as a symbol of grief in cymberline, and called it "the stinking Elder." Many people dislike the strong heady scent of its blossom, which, like the hawthorn, became associated with enchantment and witchcraft. The elder, with all its ancient associations and lineage, is not used in British heraldry, neither has it been adopted as plant badge by the Gaelic clans.

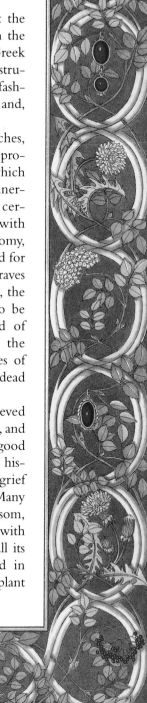

In the *Materia Medica* the elder is listed as an important herbal, with every part bearing medicinal properties—the bark, leaves, flowers, and berries all have active chemical constituents. Indeed, the elder is one of the few plants that has maintained its value from earliest times; the berries were eaten in Neolithic times, and the therapeutic value of its flowers and fruits was known to the Druids.

During the month of the thirteenth sign the last berries were picked with solemn rites. The wine made from these berries was considered the last sacred gift of their Earth goddess, not to be drunk by common folk, but only by the initiated priesthood; it was said to produce the most powerful hallucinations, and could therefore be used in their arcane ceremonies for prophecy and divination. It was also poured in sacred places, and drunk by the sacrificial victims at the time of the solstices to help regenerate both the body and the spirit.

Ruis

This is the Ogham letter word for the month of the elder, a month when the wave returns to the sea, marking the end of the year as it returns to its watery beginning, as recorded in the *Song of Amergin*. A wave of the sea in Irish and Welsh poetry is a sea-stag; the year thus symbolically begins and ends with the white roebuck. In the Irish legend of Cuchulain and Fionn they fought the wave with a sword and spear.

Astrological Significance

In Celtic astrology, the winter solstice marked the beginning of Arthur's season, when he was engaged in fighting the powers of darkness who were more potently active during the last two winter months. He symbolically represented the Sun or solar spirit, and was depicted as the archer, armed with a bow and arrow to combat the darkness of winter. The Earth was known as the Three Queens of Arthur, who presided over spring, summer, and autumn. The evil principles were the three male energies, of Avagddu, Cythraul, and Atrais—in Druidism the three energies or spirits affecting human nature, and which required dispersing or absorbing. Arthur appears to be the Celtic equivalent to the Archetypal Man, and the Arthurian legends provide a source of great insight into the British psyche.

Saturn is the astrological ruler of this sign. Its traditional association with the winter solstice in the Graeco-Roman zodiac, as a time lord, also fits into the mythological format of the Druidic lunar zodiac. Time and space as a dimensional plane are also constantly referred to in Celtic myths, and the realm of Annwn or the terrestrial regions appears to mark the entrance into another time and another world.

Saturn in esoteric astrology has been referred to as the subduer, an apt comparison to Arthur's role at this time of the year. Many astrologers regard Saturn as the most important planet in natal charts or horoscopes, because its position reveals a level of evolution marking the critical stage between the real and the unreal, the true and the false or, more symbolically, light and darkness of character. Saturn has three modes of expression that govern all the actions of humanity: first, he is the chief ruler over fate and destiny; second, he is the lord of the mineral kingdom, in which the source of all life and light is imprisoned; and third, he represents the highest mental attribute of perfection.

The month of the elder in the Celtic lunar zodiac is a time symbolizing the imprisonment of the Sun or solar spirit, and therefore this association with Saturn is well founded.

Archetypal Character

The mythology of the horse goddess Rhiannon that relates to this sign has already been mentioned under the sign of the oak tree (summer solstice), and reflects the polarity and integrating aspect of the elder tree character. But the archetypal character associated with this sign of the elder is Pryderi, son of the horse goddess Rhiannon, and Pwyll, god of the underworld. Pryderi was born on the day of the winter solstice and mysteriously abducted, and fostered by a kindly stranger. Pryderi, whose name means "trouble" or "care," was aptly named, for his disappearance caused his mother to suffer an unjust penance and a loss of faith in the integrity of the goddess. This relates to the struggle for supremacy between the solar and lunar deities.

Pryderi was eventually restored, however, and, with his friend Manannan, accompanied Bran on his mission to restore his sister Branwen to her rightful position in Ireland. In the battle that ensued, Bran was slain and Pryderi and Manannan were among the few survivors who brought Bran's head back to Britain for burial. On their return they were confronted by new insurgent forces, an invasion of continental Celts. Pryderi was eventually slain by the magic of Gwydion, a god of science and light, which again suggests the battle for supremacy between the old gods and foreign ones. Pryderi therefore represents the uncertainty of life and the need for constant adjustments associated with elder tree people; his powers of survival, however, represent another important facet of character.

Tree Character

Elder tree characters command respect, exerting a powerful influence as they grow older. In their youth they are extravagant in every sense, and inclined to waste much time and energy. People born under this sign often have a sense of fatalism that they try to resist, like the reed characters, but it holds great sway in their actions and subconscious mind. However, the ability to comprehend the complexities of life finally dawns, and the gift of understanding is the culmination of wisdom and a lapsed faith, although they must travel far or search hard to find it.

Some notable elder tree characters include Mary, Queen of Scots, Sir Winston Churchill, Beethoven, and Disraeli.

Positive Aspects

They have a constructive approach to life. They will continue a struggle that would defeat most people, even the powerful reed characters. They have a certain patience and self-discipline, but their real strength lies in their instinctive knowledge of when they are right and other people are in the wrong.

Negative Aspects

They can be heartless and cruel people. They may became involved in public scandals because of their lack of judgment in their choice of friends and by allowing their personal ambitions to dominate, for they are highly ambitious people who are determined to win at all costs.

General

Their search for fame and fortune will take them to many foreign places, only to discover that their destiny lies much closer to home. The study of ancient cultures and philosophies will be their guide, but a restless spirit prevails. Of all the signs, the elder tree characters require the most understanding. In the early days they put on a convincing show of not really taking things too seriously, but they are inevitably drawn into more powerful arenas or contests by their personal convictions. Unlike the reed people, who seek personal power, elder people are dogmatic characters who enjoy challenging the power of the land or what they see as great injustices.

Being outspoken people, they are at times inclined to speak without thinking deeply enough, which can become the easy way out of a situation. And if they speak bluntly enough, people will learn to keep their distance. But they have, nevertheless, the ability to sway people with great oratory when they so choose. Elder tree characters are in the same mold as the brave oak people, their opposite sign and polarity, but the elder tree people are the constantly misunderstood people of the Celtic lunar zodiac.

They are very energetic people who can be seen jogging around the park in the early hours in all weathers. Their physical stamina is hyperactive; they usually become involved with outdoor sports or activities, and this may attract them into a professional sporting career. Military careers are also top of the list, and that urge for travel promotes journalists as well as sports promoters and commentators. This is the extrovert elder tree character at its best—finger on the button, ready to fire the questions, exerting a high profile. Perhaps it is not surprising that they often end up in politics.

The quieter type of elder tree character is less obvious, but remains a powerful figure, even on the sidelines. For no one can dodge or avoid their responsibilities forever, even though such elder characters may appear to make a good show at trying. They make staunch friends and teammates, for they have the cheek of the devil and will never let the side down.

Love Life

Their personal lives are an open book. They will saunter away from the most disastrous relationships as if they were only bystanders, this casual attitude being their hallmark or notoriety. Do they ever really fall in love with any of their willing victims? Occasionally they do, especially in the very first moments of a relationship. But they are not heartless people, however, just overly romantic and lustful.

They make wonderful aunts and uncles, who bring back the most exciting souvenirs of their travels, with incredible stories to tell. They also make ideal parents if the opportunity arises, but even when married they will never be around all the time because of their careers and restless nature.

Summary

The most enduring part of their nature is their sense of humor, which can become rather black on ccasion. But it will score a hit for the whole of humanity when directed at false prophets and merchants of doom. Their lifestyle is quite different from everyone else's. They will dine with kings and queens and then take a nightcap with a passing tramp. Is it a protest against society or themselves? Whatever, they will keep the tabloids busy.

They seldom have a quiet life, enjoying the noise and bustle of the city or town as a rule, although they are equally adaptable anywhere. If it's a country life they choose, they are most likely to become the squire, with a menagerie of wild folk and animals as houseguests. But when the facade wears thinner with maturity and old age, the world is suddenly presented with one of the leading pillars of society.

THE NAMELESS DAY
December 23

The Mistletoe

This revered plant of the Druids was the emblem of life through death. The later Christian custom of kissing under the mistletoe on Christmas Eve was to promote peace. But whatever the custom or calendar, the intercalary day or extra day of the year was sacred to the Dark Queen in Celtic myth.

The Black Pearl

Natural pearls are found in oysters and clams in warm salt water throughout the world. Some river mussels also produce pearls, and Roman writers have referred to pearls being found in British rivers. Indeed, up to the last century there existed a pearl fishing industry that operated in Welsh and Scottish rivers; the British Crown jewels include items set with pearls from these rivers. Because of their unique beauty and natural form, pearls are considered as precious as diamonds. Black pearls in particular are extremely rare, almost legendary, and represent an odd phenomenon of nature. The black pearl is therefore associated with this sign as a symbol of uniqueness.

Mythology Associated with the Nameless Day

There is a separate mention for this date with regard to interpretation of character because this day in the Druidic calendar falls outside the 13-month year, and is therefore not ruled by any trees. But it has been associated with the mythology of the yew tree and the sacred mistletoe.

In Roman mythology this day was sacred to Larunda, an extremely obscure Roman goddess said to be of Sabine origin. She was honored on December 23 at an altar in Velabrium, and the ancients equated her with Lara, the mother of the Lares or household gods. Offerings were made to her on this day for the departed spirits of slaves, and the priests officially designated the day for ancestor worship. But generally speaking very little is recorded about this day in world myths, and it remains one of the mysteries of the Druidic religion.

People born on this day still come under the general vibrations of the elder tree sign, the difference being that now we have the serious "twin" to both the Sun and Moon. The number of people born on this day must run into millions worldwide, but to people of Celtic blood or ancestry this interpretation may help to provide the missing key to their whole psyche.

General Summary

These are people of solid achievement, more akin to the birch characters, with the exception of their being more charismatic. They are people who can quite literally rise from rags to riches by the sweat of their own brow, but they prefer to devote their life to the service of others. There is, however, a great mystery about these people, not unlike the reed characters; they are, it seems, very reluctant to become involved too intimately, a similar trait to that of the elder tree characters, but for altogether different reasons.

Elder tree people may be wary of family responsibility, but for people born on the twenty-third day of the thirteenth month the aversion is to the fear of failure, a fear that makes them step back rather than forward. They will therefore give much thought to both friendship and personal relationships before making any commitments. When they fall in love, it will be forever, and they are the most devoted sons and daughters in the family. Their own parents may have set high standards of achievements, which they intend to follow at all costs.

They see life clearly for what it is—a great challenge—and they distrust people who appear always to take the easier course of action, probably because they understand the penalties likely to be levied. They may also travel great distances in connection with their careers; indeed they may be born in foreign places, away from their native land, due to their parents' careers. But in later years they will return to the very same house or town to carry on family traditions or businesses. They thus represent old-fashioned values and service.

BIBLIOGRAPHY

Bailey, Alice A. *Esoteric Astrology, Vol. 3.* Lucis, New York, 1976.

Bailey, Alice A. *A Treatise on Cosmic Fire.* Lucis, New York, 1977.

Blavatsky, Helena. *The Secret Doctrine.* Gilmour & Dean, London, 1950.

Boland, Bridget. *Gardener's Magic and Other Old Wives' Lore.* W. & J. Mackay, Chatham, 1977.

Bord, Janet and Colin. *Mysterious Britain.* Paladin, London, 1974.

Burl, Aubrey. *The Stonehenge People.* Barrie & Jenkins, London, 1989.

Culpeper, Nicholas. *Culpeper's Complete Herbal.* Foulsham, London, 1952.

Cumont, Franz. *Astrology and Religion among the Greeks and Romans.* Dover, New York, 1960.

Donnelly, Ignatius. *Atlantis, the Antediluvian World.* Harper & Brothers, New York, 1882.

Eitel, Ernest J. *Feng-Shui.* Synergetic, London, 1984.

Geoffrey of Monmouth. *The History of the Kings of Britain.* Penguin, London, 1988.

Goldstein-Jacobson, Ivy M. *The Dark Moon: Lilith in Astrology.* Frank Severy, California, 1961.

Graves, Robert. *The White Goddess.* Faber & Faber, London, 1971.

Grieve, Mrs. M. *A Modern Herbal.* Penguin, London, 1980.

Guerber, H. A. *The Myths of Greece and Rome.* Harrap, London, 1909.

Halliday, F.E., *A Concise History of England,* Book Club Associates, London, 1974.

Hawkins, Gerald S. *Stonehenge Decoded.* Fontana/Collins, London, 1982.

Heaps, Willard A. *Birthstones and The Lore of Gemstones.* Angus & Robertson, London, 1971.

Howes, Michael. *Amulets.* Robert Hale, London, 1975.

Hope-Moncrieff, A. R. *Romance and Legend of Chivalry.* Gresham, London, 1948.

Hope, Murry. *Practical Celtic Magic.* Aquarian, Wellingborough, 1987.

Jones, Gwyn and Thomas. *The Mabinogion.* Dent, London, 1978.

Leo, Alan. *The Art of Synthesis,* Fowler, London, 1968.

Lockhart, J. G. *Curses, Lucks and Talismans.* Geoffrey Bles, London, 1938.

Logan, Patrick. *Irish Country Cures.* Appletree, Belfast, 1981.

MacGregor, Alexander. *Highland Superstitions.* Eneas Mackay, Scotland, 1951.

Mclean, Adam. *The Four Fire Festivals.* Megalithic Research, Edinburgh, 1979.

Matthews, Caitlin. *The Celtic Tradition.* Element, Shaftesbury, 1989.

Moore, Patrick. *The Observer's Book of Astronomy.* Frederick Warne, London, 1978.

O'Kelly, Michael J. *Newgrange Archaeology, Art and Legend.* Thames & Hudson, London, 1982.

Rees, Alwyn and Brinley. *Celtic Heritage.* Thames & Hudson, London, 1989.

Robertson-Durdin, Lawrence. *Perpetual Calendar of the Fellowship of Isis.* Cesara, Enniscorthy, Eire, 1982.

Rolleston, T. W. *Myths and Legends of the Celtic Race.* Harrap, London, 1917.

Semple, William. *The Scottish Tartans.* W. & A. K. Johnston, Scotland.

Spence, Lewis. *The Mysteries of Britain.* Society of Metaphysicians, 1986.

Vogh, James. *Arachne Rising.* Granada, London, 1977.

Volguine, Alexandre. *Lunar Astrology.* Asi, New York, 1974.

de Vore, Nicholas. *Encyclopedia of Astrology.* Littlefield, Adams, New York, 1977.

Walters, W. D. *Wonderful Herbal Remedies.* Celtic Educational, 1979.

Weston, L. H. *The Planet Vulcan.* American Federation of Astrologers, Arizona.

REFERENCE SOURCES

Bailey, Alice A. *Esoteric Astrology, Vol. 3.* Lucis, New York, 1976: Chapter 1, The Zodiac and the Rays, last five lines of page 12 and first line of page 13; Appendix, Planets, Rays and Esoteric Teaching, Uranus, last two lines on page 693.

Blavatsky, Helena. *The Secret Doctrine.* Gilmour & Dean, London, 1950: Western Speculations, four lines of third paragraph on page 406, Vol. 3.

Graves, Robert. *The White Goddess.* Faber & Faber, London, 1971: Chapter 12, "The Song of Amergin," revised poem of letter months, 13 lines starting on page 207.

Rolleston, T. W. *Myths and Legends of the Celtic Race.* Harrap, London, 1917: Doom of the Children of Lir, four lines, page 140.

Spence, Lewis. *The Mysteries of Britain.* Society of Metaphysicians: Chapter 4, Barddas, the enigma of the Bards, 18 lines on page 99.

STAY IN TOUCH. . .

Llewellyn publishes hundreds of books on your favorite subjects.

Your local bookstore stocks most of these books and will stock new Llewellyn titles as they become available. We urge your patronage.

ORDER BY PHONE

Call toll-free within the U.S. and Canada, **1–800–THE MOON.**

In Minnesota call **(612) 291–1970.**

We accept Visa, MasterCard, and American Express.

ORDER BY MAIL

Send the full price of your order (MN residents add 7% sales tax) in U.S. funds to:

Llewellyn Worldwide
P.O. Box 64383, Dept. K510-X
St. Paul, MN 55164–0383, U.S.A.

POSTAGE AND HANDLING

- ◆ $4.00 for orders $15.00 and under
- ◆ $5.00 for orders over $15.00
- ◆ No charge for orders over $100.00

We ship UPS in the continental United States. We ship standard mail to P.O. boxes. Orders shipped to Alaska, Hawaii, the Virgin Islands, and Puerto Rico will be sent first-class mail.

Orders shipped to Canada and Mexico are sent surface mail.

International orders: Airmail—add freight equal to price of each book to the total price of order, plus $5.00 for each non-book item (audiotapes, etc.). Surface mail: Add $1.00 per item.

Allow 4–6 weeks delivery on all orders. Postage and handling rates subject to change.

GROUP DISCOUNTS

We offer a 20% quantity discount to group leaders or agents. You must order a minimum of 5 copies of the same book to get our special quantity price.

FREE CATALOG

Get a free copy of our color catalog, *New Worlds of Mind and Spirit*. Subscribe for just $10.00 in the United States and Canada ($30.00 overseas, airmail). Many bookstores carry *New Worlds*—ask for it!